PIMLICO

590

INJURY TIME

Born in 1920, educated at Leamington College and Downing College, Cambridge, D. J. Enright spent over twenty years teaching English at universities in Egypt, Japan, Berlin, Thailand, and Singapore. He returned to London in 1970 and later became a director of London publishers Chatto & Windus.

First and foremost a poet, he published many collections in over fifty years, including *Collected Poems: 1948–98* (1998), and translations from Japanese and German verse. He wrote novels for both adults and children, and revised with Madeleine Enright the English translation of Proust's *In Search of Lost Time* (1992), while his enormous output of non-fiction includes his *Memoirs of a Mendicant Professor* (1969), a number of critical works, and several anthologies, among them *The Oxford Book of Death* (1983) and *The Faber Book of Fevers and Frets* (1989). Observations on life (high and low), literature, morals and manners, human or animal, are recorded in *The Way of the Cat* (1992), and two companion volumes to *Injury Time – Interplay: A Kind of Commonplace Book* (1995) and *Play Resumed: A Journal* (1999).

D. J. Enright received the Cholmondeley Award in 1974; he was awarded the Queen's Gold Medal for Poetry in 1981 and appointed OBE in 1991. Fellow of the Royal Society of Literature since 1961, he was made Companion of Literature by the Society in 1998, an honour granted to no more than ten living writers at any one time.

He died on the last day of 2002, after battling vigorously against cancer for seven years. As D. J. Taylor wrote in the *Times Literary Supplement*, 'Whether as poet, critic, novelist or in any of his other professional guises, he was a unique figure in recent English literary life, and we are all of us – Young Turk, grey eminence, writer and reader – diminished by his passing.'

INJURY TIME

A Memoir

D. J. ENRIGHT

PIMLICO

Published by Pimlico 2003

2 4 6 8 10 9 7 5 3 1

Copyright © The Estate of D. J. Enright 2003

Introduction copyright © John Gross 2003

D. J. Enright has asserted his right under the Copyright, Designs
and Patents Act 1988 to be identified as the author of this work

Excerpt from *Trains of Thought* by Victor Brombert reproduced by
kind permission of W.W. Norton & Company

First published in Great Britain by
Pimlico 2003

Pimlico
Random House, 20 Vauxhall Bridge Road,
London SW1V 2SA

Random House Australia (Pty) Limited
20 Alfred Street, Milsons Point, Sydney,
New South Wales 2061, Australia

Random House New Zealand Limited
18 Poland Road, Glenfield
Auckland 10, New Zealand

Random House (Pty) Limited
Endulini, 5A Jubilee Road, Parktown 2193, South Africa

The Random House Group Limited Reg. No. 954009
www.randomhouse.co.uk

A CIP catalogue record for this book
is available from the British Library

ISBN 1–8441–3315–X

Papers used by Random House are natural,
recyclable products made from wood grown in sustainable forests;
the manufacturing processes conform to the environmental
regulations of the country of origin

Typeset by Deltatype Ltd, Birkenhead, Merseyside

Printed and bound in Great Britain by
Mackays of Chatham

INTRODUCTION

Injury Time is D. J. Enright's last book, completed shortly before his death in December 2002. It marks the end of a career notable not only for originality and accomplishment, but for variety as well. Enright was a poet, critic, novelist, reviewer, children's author, translator and anthologist. He wrote a memorable book about Japan, *The World of Dew*, and an outstanding autobiography, *Memoirs of a Mendicant Professor*. And he ended up with three works – *Injury Time* and its two predecessors, *Interplay* and *Play Resumed* – which are hard to classify. He himself subtitled *Interplay* 'A Kind of Commonplace Book', *Play Resumed* 'A Journal' and *Injury Time* 'A Memoir'. In an earlier age they might have been called something like 'musings'.

Faced with this diversity, more than one obituarist was moved to describe him as a man of letters. This is a useful label applied in moderation, but one wouldn't want to make too much of it. It suggests a servant of literature rather than a creator. It draws attention away from the fact that he was above all else a poet.

A poet who maintained a high level, and who demands – or at any rate deserves – to be read in bulk. His *Collected Poems* runs to some 400 pages. Open it almost anywhere, and you will find something arresting or enlivening; something to cherish.

His poetry is marked by a number of paradoxes. In many respects, for instance, it makes a point of being anti-literary. The predominant tone is plain and colloquial. There is a constant appeal to 'life', as opposed to fine notions, and to the primacy of human beings over myths. Yet the poems are also strewn with literary references. Two collections, *Paradise Illustrated* and *A Faust Book*, take the form of verse commentaries on other men's masterpieces – *Paradise Lost* and Goethe's *Faust* respectively. (With a lesser writer such undertakings might seem bookish and derivative, but not here.) Even in his most personal and least intellectual poem, the childhood sequence *The Terrible Shears*, he permits himself an unexplained allusion of a decidedly highbrow order – to Leverkühn, in Thomas Mann's *Doktor Faustus*. The literature and life which are played off against each other in his work are also mixed together.

Again, to consider him in an international context is to be left with a double image: the citizen of the world, the man next door. He has a breadth, a freedom from insularity, which is very impressive – all the more so in comparison with the narrowness of contemporaries such as Philip Larkin and Kingsley Amis, with whom he was once (in the days of the Movement) misleadingly associated. At the most obvious level this range can be accounted for by the simple geographical facts of a teaching career which took him to Egypt, Japan, Germany, Thailand and Singapore, and kept him out of England until he was fifty. More significantly, wherever he worked he displayed an openness, a curiosity about culture, an appreciation of the extent to which the lives of the local population were ordinary as well as different. But none of this made him a cosmopolitan, which seems exactly the wrong word for him. He was too rooted. The flavour of his personality remained inescapably English.

Of all the seeming contradictions in his work, the most striking is the discrepancy between his sombre moral concerns and his lightness of touch. His poetry reveals an exceptional awareness of the human capacity for hurting and being hurt. The thought of the twentieth century's great atrocities is never very far away. He won't allow himself to forget the realities of hunger, poverty, oppression. Yet he also contrives to be wonderfully entertaining. Among the English poets of his time, I would say, only Betjeman and Gavin Ewart surpass him in this respect.

His gift is best summed up by the little word 'wit' – a word, like 'sex', that often seems too small for the burdens it has to carry. At its best, without losing its power to amuse, it means understanding, insight, a sense of irony, an ability to make connections. Enright's wit is generally of this superior kind; his comedy rests on a bedrock of seriousness. Take the short poem 'Unlawful Assembly' (the assembly was dispersed by the Singapore police). It is full of verbal ingenuities, but every pun in it makes a point, down to the final sad shrug:

> Why subscribe to clarity?
> In this vale of teargas
> Should one enter a caveat,
> Or a monastery?

Some Enright jokes, on the other hand, are there for their own sake. There was a strong element in him of pure comedian (people often said he *looked* like a comedian). He had the gift of making his readers laugh out loud. And though he sometimes gave signs of wondering whether his humour wasn't at odds with his subject-matter, this was one of the quarrels with himself out of which he made his poetry. The impulse to clown had a way of breaking through, whether he liked it or not. But then anger, affection and a whole range of other emotions had a way of breaking through the clowning.

The early poems established his credentials as a liberal, a humanist and a democrat – well aware, like all the best liberals, humanists and democrats, of his creeds' limitations. Sometimes he recalls E. M. Forster: the title of one of his early collections, *Some Men Are Brothers*, makes a perfect pair with *Two Cheers for Democracy*. And he doesn't underestimate the madness of the world:

> (You think it is easy, all this sanity?
> Try it. It will send you mad.)

But he isn't actually giving up on sanity. The comment is only a parenthesis.

In the later poems there is an increasing preoccupation with religion. Not so much with religion itself as with the sense of religion, or the empty space that religion has left behind. The brilliantly funny contrasts in *Paradise Illustrated* cut both ways. The myths are antiquated, the shallow colloquial idiom points up what has been lost:

> 'Death,' said Adam in funereal tones.
> 'That's the worst of what we have done.
> As for the rest of it – that's life.
> But Death's a killer.'

At the same time, there is no suggestion that God, if He exists, is ready to vouchsafe the answers:

> Too weak to shiver, children die of cold.
> God moves, unmoved, in mysterious ways ...

But the human reaching out for God can be very moving.

What the poems fail to achieve (how many poems do?) is maximum verbal intensity. A few come close to it: some of the Japanese poems, *The Terrible Shears*. Many others feature subtle stylistic or rhythmic effects: they are far from being the loose jottings which detractors claim. But they don't create a sense of absolute unalterable precision. Enright isn't a poet who shows up at his best in anthologies. You have to read his poems in their natural setting to see quite how good they are.

That still leaves his mastery of prose. A tour of his prose writings which did them justice would linger over such landmarks as his sparkling defence of irony, *The Alluring Problem*, and the fine serio-comic novel he wrote about Alexandria, *Academic Year* (published in 1955, rediscovered in the 1980s and surely due to be rediscovered again). It would pay tribute not only to *Memoirs of a Mendicant Professor* but also to *Shakespeare and the Students* (an introduction to four of the plays which give you a vivid idea of what his virtues as a professor must have been). And it would pause to salute the most notable of his anthologies, *The Oxford Book of Friendship*, *The Oxford Book of the Supernatural* and *The Oxford Book of Death*. They are not just compilations but imaginative works in their own right – what Ezra Pound called 'active anthologies'.

He was also an outstanding reviewer-cum-essayist. The most substantial of his critical essays were gathered together over the years in three collections: *Conspirators and Poets*, *Man Is an Onion*, *A Mania for Sentences*. They include some particularly useful studies of German authors – Hölderlin, Thomas Mann, Hugo von Hofmannsthal, Günter Grass and others: vigorous assessments which allow for the possibility that many British readers may have resistances which have to be overcome. (A general set of reflections, 'Aimez-vous Goethe?', carries the deadpan subtitle 'An Enquiry into English Attitudes of Non-liking Towards German Literature'.) But all the literary pieces are distinguished by humanity and good sense. They take stock of subjects ranging from Nabokov to Mishima, from Aleister Crowley to Stevie Smith – always with verve, though sometimes with less than total respect. A consideration of Simone de Beauvoir's essay on the Marquis de Sade. 'Must We Burn Sade?', offers the thought: 'Must we burn Sade? Now that you mention it, why not?'

Beyond these essays lie the hundreds of minor reviews which Enright published, and which are presumably never going to be collected. It's a fate which has to be bowed to: not everything can be saved. But a great deal of admirable writing is going to be lost with them – beautifully apt formulations, illuminating asides, devastating (but never brutal) judgements, common sense delivered with epigrammatic force. Some of Enright's remarks I find myself recalling years afterwards, long after the occasion for them has faded. His response when he was reviewing a dodgy biographical study of Thomas Hardy, for instance, and the author asked whether the events described in such and such a Hardy poem actually happened: 'They happen every time you read it.'

In *Interplay* (1995) many of Enright's gifts came together. It is a hotchpotch (his own word for it) which also doubles as an anthology and a collection of miniature essays. It contains anecdotes, squibs, aphorisms, reminiscences, timeless thoughts, topical notes, comic turns, unfamiliar quotations. There are even a few poems.

At seventy-five Enright had discovered a form of writing which suited him perfectly. Perhaps it wouldn't have worked so well for him when he was younger: the book very much reflects his advanced and advancing years. Not, one hastens to add, in any diminution of energy or acuteness. It is wonderfully lively. In some respects – in its reactions to news items and television programmes, for instance – it might even be called strikingly up to date. But it is also a work of long perspectives, of judgements tempered by a lifetime's experience. Much of it is devoted to the condition of old age itself. And the fact that Enright went on living in the present didn't oblige him to like the present. The book is also part polemic, part sottisier. It sets its face against false fashions and approved-of brutalities, against the coarsening and dehumanizing of contemporary life.

One must be careful. It is easy for old men to idealize the past, easy for them to attribute their own infirmities to the times they live in, easy for them to interpret any change as a threat. Enright was well aware of these dangers. He frequently reverts to them. But by and large he trusts his own reactions. And he provides evidence. Many of his quotations and examples are hilarious, especially when they involve mangled language. Others, in principle at least, are depressing:

> The television listing says of a documentary: '. . . offers that awful cliché, a message of hope'. Most of the rest of the evening's viewing has to do with murder, sexual problems, sick comedy. No mention of awful clichés there.

By itself, that could make you feel rather glum. But the quality of Enright's attack is bracing. So, emphatically, is the book as a whole.

Three years later, *Play Resumed* offered more of the same – which is exactly what Enright's admirers had hoped for. So, up to a point, does the present book. It is as fresh and attractive as its predecessors. But it is also shadowed, much more directly, by death. Illness is one of its central themes.

When I began reading the manuscript, only a week or two after Enright died, I felt melancholy and apprehensive. The melancholy didn't go away: almost every page brought home how sad it was, and how frustrating, that one wasn't going to be able to speak to this man again. But I can only report that as I read on, my most obvious reaction was laughter – one little explosion after another. *Injury Time* seems to me the funniest of the three final books, though I can't quite say why. Possibly it's pure chance. Possibly, near the end, Enright's perception of human folly grew even sharper.

Certainly his exasperation is unabated. Corruptions of language are put on display alongside corruptions of manners: often the two are inseparable. The universities receive some particularly satisfying swipes (their fund-raising techniques no less than the nonsenses which prevail in English Departments). So, inevitably, does journalism. The triumphs of ignorance and the failures of sensitivity (or plain decency) are tracked down in many other quarters.

This is only one strand in the book, however. For the most part curiosity and pleasure in quirkiness get the better of pessimism. Distaste for bad writing is matched – surpassed – by the love of good writing. Small beguiling anecdotes jostle with reflections on large issues – on the Self, on whether anything matters. You are repeatedly impressed (though he himself would have groaned at the word) by Enright's wisdom.

And then, in a region where wisdom is only of limited help, there are the ravages of illness. Enright doesn't say much about them, and we are grateful for his reserve. But of course he says something, and there are enough glimpses to give us some notion of his multiple ordeal. (A mention of twisted arthritic fingers pulls us up short. That too: we hadn't realized . . .) There are also plentiful reminders that 'patient' will always be, as he says, 'a demeaning word'. It's no reflection on the care we receive. It's just the way things are.

Mostly, though, we are struck by his determination to go on living life on his own terms as long as he humanly can. The book increasingly comes to seem a victory over the illness; and to that extent it is not only a wise book, and an entertaining one, but a heroic book as well.

John Gross

ACKNOWLEDGEMENTS

The author wishes to thank his daughter Dominique Enright, her husband Toby Buchan, and Gertrude Watson for their great help in preparing this manuscript.

Many of you will not have lived before. You would never have dreamt of it. Now you are living, and we hope that you will enjoy it. But it is our responsibility to warn you that LIFE CAN GO DOWN IN VALUE AS WELL AS UP, and the past is not a sure guide to the future. Living can be bad for your well-being and even lead to death.

From 'Warnings, warnings!'
(*Old Men and Comets*, 1993)

I am always sorry when any language is lost, because languages are the pedigree of nations.

Samuel Johnson

Next in criminality to him who violates the laws of his country, is he who violates the language.

Walter Savage Landor

Diseases crucify the soul of man, attenuate our bodies, dry them, wither them, shrivel them up like old apples, make them so many anatomies.

Robert Burton

Take heed, sickness, what you do:
I shall fear you'll surfeit too.
Live not we as all thy stalls,
Spitals, pest-houses, hospitals,
Scarce will take our present store?
And this age will build no more.

Ben Jonson

Illness is the night-side of life, a more onerous citizenship. Everyone who is born holds dual citizenship, in the kingdom of the well and in the kingdom of the sick. Although we all prefer to use only the good passport, sooner or later each of us is obliged, at least for a spell, to identify ourselves as citizens of that other place.

Susan Sontag

I write to Gale Research Inc., Detroit, to ask that any future requests to reprint material should be addressed to *me*, not to my literary estate. (See, if so inclined, *Play Resumed*, p. 199.) Next I buy a handsome A4 Feint notebook, Tiger Brand, from Ryman, hoping that notes will follow. A label says 'Discontinued'. Is this a hint? A paper tiger? (Superstition, said Goethe, is the poetry of life. No, rather the foolish, shamefaced, harsh, implacable doggerel of one's declining years.) And then 'feint', surely a good omen; defined in the dictionaries as ruled paper 'with inconspicuous lines to guide writing' – i.e. discreet inspiration.

C. H. Sisson has a poem, 'Looking at Old Note-Books', which begins: 'It would seem that I thought,/ At that time, more than I ought.' No danger of that here; this is a new notebook. Later in the poem: 'There was the London Library/ Doing its best to confuse me.' That doesn't apply either, except that the Library lifts confuse me and the stairs forbid. An impoverishment of one's life. Long ago, when searching out items for an anthology on the subject of Death, I fell over an invisible stool, stumbled against the bookstack, and dislodged a number of volumes which fell on the other side of the stack. A cry of distress arose, and I hurried round to find a frail young woman lying on the floor, covered in books. Apologizing, I scooped up the books and restored them to their putative places on the shelves. The young woman, recovering her wits, snapped out:

'You've put back the books I want to take out!' I limped away, feeling a trickle of warm liquid down my leg. Blood, it turned out. And a long tear in my trousers. Those were the days.

Ministers of (or for) Culture used to be figures of fun or of fear, known for their bumbling pronouncements or their close association with the secret police. Nowadays they are as respectable as other Ministers, neither made sport of nor trembled at. Their company is eagerly sought by a multitude of citizens concerned in one way or another with the hazy, low-ranking but sometimes pleasurable responsibilities grouped together as 'culture', and ranging from poets looking for patrons to aspiring pop stars with relatively undemanding sports persons in the middle. What might this phenomenon portend? The onset of a golden age?

It is reported in the press that a spokesman for the Hell's Angels has a Ph.D. in motorcycle culture from Warwick University: presumably an aspect of the 'car culture' and 'philosophy of road traffic' about which we hear so much. Also in the news is the 'drug culture', the 'culture of violence', the 'teenage knife culture', the 'culture of cover-up', the thriving 'compensation culture' (as the television jingle goes: 'Where there's blame there's a claim'), and the 'credit-card culture'. Recently an American spokeswoman, on the defensive, has insisted that al-Qaeda fighters held in the US prison camp in Cuba are being served 'culturally appropriate food', while Mr Duncan Smith, Tory leader, accuses the British Government and National Health Service doctors of joining in a 'culture of deceit', and Oxford University Press publishes a scholarly volume entitled *The Culture of Control: Crime and Social Order in Contemporary Society*.

The clear majority of these cultures are less than unequivocally desirable; we don't hear of a 'culture of kindness', or of 'teenage fellowship', a 'savings bank culture', or a 'culture of openness'. It's all a long way from Matthew Arnold's idea of culture as that which aspired 'to make all men live in an atmosphere of sweetness and light'.

'I'd like to know whether epochs that possessed culture knew the word at all, or used it': thus the young Adrian Leverkühn, in Mann's *Doctor Faustus*.

The Age of – what? Of Bad Causes, since all the Good Causes seem to have gone off. 'I put it down to these officious Modern Communications,' says the old fellow. 'In the old days we didn't *know* so much about other people. We took them as we found them, those we did find, not all that many. It sort of *helped*.' God help us, he added hopefully. All that poncing around on the telly! Worse today, but not altogether new. He thinks of two defining moments in the history of (that word again) culture. Ulrich was more or less used to hearing about 'geniuses of the football field or the boxing ring', but was still taken aback by the phrase 'the racehorse of genius' (Robert Musil, 1930). And 'We are intimate with people we have never seen and, unhappily, they are intimate with us. Democritus plucked his eye out because he could not look at a woman without thinking of her as a woman. If he had read a few of our novels, he would have torn himself to pieces' (Wallace Stevens, 1942).

A reviewer in the *Times Literary Supplement* has remarked on my addiction to 'dreadful puns'. Surely 'one of the most excruciating', he says, is the doubt as to 'whether one exorcizes one's fears by writing about them, or exercises them'. He could have done better than that, for I have certainly done worse. After all, it's not an egregiously disembodied, gratuitous piece of word play; the thought may not be gloriously original, but it's clear and, where 'meaning' is concerned, plausible. (Ah, but 'plausible' is synonymous with 'glib' and 'specious'.)

Now, some six weeks later, I see in the *Hampstead and Highgate Express* a review of André Dubus's *Dancing After Hours*: 'With these stories he seems to be exorcizing demons. Or, rather, exercising them.' Well done, Guy Somerset! I hope you get away with it.

The electronic notice-board reads 'WELCOME TO ACCIDENT AND EMERGENCY'. Below: 'WAITING TIME MAJOR INJURIES 4 HOURS . . . MINOR INJURIES 4 HOURS', followed by running information, broken by occasional lacunae, about the more serious cases being treated before the less, and on how to procure food and drink while waiting and a taxi to take one home. The Coca-Cola dispensers are built like tanks; many of the foam-rubber seats have suffered major injuries.

'Welcome to Accident and Emergency.' One might wish to respond with the Psalmist's words: 'Give ear unto my cry, for I am a stranger with thee, and a sojourner. O spare me, that I may recover strength, before I go hence, and be no more.'

No trouble with the hospital computer this time; no vain search for an Enwright. Thanks no doubt to the BBC's Dublin reporter, Leo Enright, whose genial face, subtitled by his name, is often seen on television these days.

I was pleased that Anthony Burgess spelt the name correctly in his novel, *Earthly Powers*. Even though he gave it to a catamite. (The latter word deriving from a Trojan prince called Ganymede, beloved of Zeus.)

In fact there isn't a long wait. The electronic notice-board was on the blink, waiting for treatment.

'Great physical languor, especially in the morning. It is Calvary to get out of bed and shoulder the day's burden.

' "What's been the matter?" they ask.

' "Oh! senile decay – general histolysis of the tissues," I say, fencing': W. N. P. Barbellion, 1914, *aetat.* twenty-five. His doctor tells him these waves of ill health are quite unaccountable, unless he is leading a dissolute life, which he doesn't appear to be doing. 'Damn his eyes.'

'Beware of desp'rate steps. The darkest day/ (Live till tomorrow) will have pass'd away'. William Cowper, that educated hypochondriac, on 'The Needless Alarm'.

At my age, every trivial twinge seems a harbinger of dissolution. Yet there is a sort of safety in numbers. Variety is the spice of life? More certainly, variety is the spice of death.

The most overblown understatement of the week: 'One could call Swift the Peter Mandelson of his day, but that is only half the story' (*Daily Telegraph*).

The mystery of market values. A hairdresser in Florida is offering Monica Lewinsky $100,000 for her blue cocktail dress allegedly bearing traces of President Clinton's semen. (Remember that sweet song, 'These foolish things remind me of you'?) And $100,000 would buy a lifetime's supply of condoms.

People had a strange feeling that they were more than they seemed, or could be better than they were. And so religion came into the world. Now religion is going out of the world, our world. We understand that we are less than we seem, and can easily be worse than we possibly are.

The book is sickening. I try to put it down, the cover sticks to my hands. I have to wash them. The book shouldn't be read, it shouldn't have been published, it shouldn't have been written. It's making money – there's no more to be said.

Which won't prevent us from saying more. There are books – novels, 'the one bright book of life'! – that one hurries through, spending time that ought to be spent on other things. Not that one is enjoying them, far from it. The going is sickening, one has to see it through to the inevitably nauseating end, and get rid of it, in accord with some perverse notion of readerly honour. Not transported – transfixed. 'I couldn't put the book down' sometimes means 'I wish I hadn't picked the book up.'

David Hume was far from supposing that 'all those, who have depreciated our species, have been enemies to virtue'. He was aware that 'a delicate sense of morals, especially when attended with a splenetic temper, is apt to give a man a disgust of the world'. However, he was of the opinion that 'the sentiments of those, who are inclined to think favourably of mankind, are more advantageous to virtue, than the contrary principles, which give us a mean opinion of our nature', for if a man holds 'a high notion of his rank and character in the creation, he will naturally endeavour to act up to it': 'On the Dignity or Meanness of Human Nature', 1741. (I now see that William James was of a like opinion: there are cases where faith creates its own verification.)

True, believing something may help to make it come true. It's harder, no doubt, to think favourably of mankind. You don't need a splenetic temper, merely access to the media, whose servants know that vice has far more to offer than virtue. Even so, one must detest and dissent from those who, in the manifest absence of any delicate sense of morals, prosper by promulgating a low opinion of our species and a disgust of the world. Believing something can help to make it come true.

One of the alarming considerations that arise in age ... Sydney Smith calculated that between the ages of ten and seventy he had eaten and drunk forty four-horse wagonloads of meat and drink *more* than would have served to keep him in good health. The cost of this surfeit came to £7,000. And it struck him that by his voracity he must have starved to death at least a hundred persons. A cheque to Oxfam seems indicated.

*

'Ah, Doctor, gout – the only enemy I do not wish to have at my feet.' It is unwise to joke with the medical profession. On the first occasion you may escape with a blank look, and on the second with a cold one. On the third you risk being struck off the doctor's list. When Smith was unwell, his doctor told him to take a walk on an empty stomach. 'Whose?' he asked. To get away with such impertinence, you will need to be the privileged patient of a private practitioner.

Smith found his friend Lady Grey guilty of anti-egotism because she would never speak of her health. 'When I am ill,' he said, 'I mention it to all my friends and relations, to the lord lieutenant of the county, the justices, the bishop, the churchwardens, the booksellers and editors of the *Edinburgh* and *Quarterly* reviews.' A sign of rude health, I'd say.

To promote a visit by the Budapest Gypsy Symphony Orchestra to Dorking in early 2002, the proud local council sent out a mailshot to 25,000 residents. Sydney Smith's witticism concerning gout may conceivably have inspired the PRO responsible for the wording: the concert promised to be 'the only time you want to see 100 Gypsies on your doorstep'. Twenty-five thousand apologies followed.

The soaps are in a lather – *EastEnders* has featured homosexuals and a bisexual, but now *Coronation Street* acquires a transsexual! – and the water grows ever murkier. Sweet Sally Webster is having an affair – or is it an optical illusion? (Actually the transsexual is an outstandingly decent and likeable character. May she stay the course.)

Have written just one sentence this fine day. (This sentence.) Feel lazy. Pick up 'Real Life' section of newspaper. Eye falls on horoscope: 'You are working too hard.' Hastily discard newspaper.

(Still, have written six, no, seven sentences now, albeit rather short ones.)

Abandoning belief, Emily Dickinson wrote, made behaviour small: 'better an ignis fatuus than no illume at all'. 'All Faith, they say, is like a jewel,' Gavin Ewart has observed, 'but why is it so bloody cruel?' Ugo Betti has submitted that to believe in something you also have to believe in everything necessary for believing in it.

The Lambeth Conference, 1998: an unseemly spat develops between the African bishops and their Western colleagues – one of whom describes the former as 'just one step up from witchcraft'. The Africans hold certain beliefs. They believe that homosexuality is wrong, 'a white man's disease'. (They may well believe – I don't know whether the point was made explicitly – that gay rights don't count for very much beside the right of black children not to die of starvation.) The Bishop of Newark, defender of a different faith, believes himself to be 'a twentieth-century person' (nothing, one might think, to boast about), free of superstition (the Virgin Birth, the Resurrection), and claims to have thirty homosexual priests in his diocese. (No nonsense there about one's belief requiring one to believe in everything deemed necessary to believing in that belief.) In a separate development, we hear of a Nigerian missionary who has come to Britain to rescue the country from 'the dark forces of humanism'. (At last someone is taking humanism seriously.) As the last English gentleman is expected to be an Indian, so it seems the last Anglican bishop is likely to be an African.

Compromises are arrived at, however, and temporizing takes precedence over eternalizing. The Conference votes to change the recommendation of 'chastity' for unmarried couples to 'abstinence'. (Which makes the heart grow fonder?) Homophobia is to be deplored, but active homosexuals are not to be ordained. Naturally, not everybody is happy. The Bishop of Edinburgh complains that he is 'gutted, shafted and depressed' (a peculiar choice of adjectives:

perhaps the Bishop is a twentieth-century person), and fears the Church is on the path to fundamentalism. (The trouble with belief is that if it isn't fundamental, it's not much of a belief.)

But the Church still stands, and with luck it will be ten years before the next Lambeth Conference. Who knows what will happen once the Africans are safely back in their native bush?

In a report of an Indian statue in the dubiously legal possession of a Birmingham museum, *The Times* Diary, 17 August 1998, is so irrationally pleased with its headline, 'Bhudda hell!' that it repeats the solecism a moment later.

The other day I asked our local florist to send flowers by Interflora to my sister, recovering from an operation. The girl in charge took the address down as 'Bomont Ward' (Beaumont), 'Warick Hospital, Warick' (Warwick). The crucial word came out 'bowkay' (bouquet) – crucial in that the only other option on offer was a wreath. Obviously the young lady, undeniably a true-born Briton, was a champion of spelling reform, and desirous of overthrowing the allegation made by Kurt Tucholsky, German satirist, that English is 'a simple but difficult language consisting entirely of foreign words mispronounced'.

'Both life and death are necessary factors of each other.' (For instance.) The moralizer goes on moralizing, the aphorist aphorizing, the ironist ironizing, the poet poetizing. News comes of a flood here, a drought there. Moralist, aphorist, ironist, poet go on doing what they do. The rescuers rescue, the aiders aid, the doctors doctor, the cobbler sticks to his last, the penman to his pen. Quite right, one says, life goes on. In fact one can think of some things that might be called life, and which ought to go on. But is writing – whether moralistic, aphoristic, ironic or poetic – one of them? Well, what can't be cured must be endured, writes the writer. (A bomb goes off in Omagh, for instance.) And feels rather pleased with himself or herself. Scraps of age-old wisdom can sound quite original when there's nothing new to say.

Whatever he did – Samuel Butler resolved – he must *not* die poor. Examples of ill-rewarded labour were immoral since they discouraged those who could and would write good things so long as they didn't fear it would ruin them and their families. Can't say the thought had ever entered my head with much force. Butler said that such examples led people to 'pamper' foolish writers out of compunction. Which may account for the ingenious and disinterested acclaim that reviewers bestow on plainly inferior books.

Of course, footballers, models, pop stars and so on didn't exist in Butler's day – all that gang, in no need of more wealth to keep them and their families from ruination, and hardly deserving it. A ghastly lust for 'knowing about' the famous, famous for no matter what, has reduced the call for compunction. As for discouragement, long banished.

Years back, in the *Sunday Times*, I volunteered the suggestion that the Arts Council should think of awarding bursaries to selected persons to enable them to give up writing. This drew a vicious letter from a man who assumed I was a Jew grown rich from contributing to what he termed the 'Sunday jewspapers'.

When Q. D. Leavis heard that I and the fellow undergraduate with whom I shared rooms had complained about the food dished out by Downing College, she rebuked us sharply: we came from working-class families and were used to our mothers' cooking, whereas if we had been sent away to public schools, we would be grateful for what Downing provided. I was reminded of this incident when reading D. J. Taylor's novel, *Trespass*, where a posh girl tells the narrator: 'It's not our fault, darling, if we weren't born with your disadvantages.'

A small, sad insight into Grub Street, in a footnote of Barbellion's:

he once received from an editor a very encouraging letter which gave him great pleasure and led him to hope that the editor was going to open the pages of his magazine to him. But three weeks later the editor committed suicide by jumping out of his bedroom window.

Janet Montefiore alerts me to Eliza Acton's *Modern Cookery* (1840), and her recipes for a Poor Author's Pudding (breadcrumbs and a few currants) and a Publisher's Pudding (soaked in cream and brandy, with crystallized fruit).

When Collins backed out of publishing *The Journal of a Disappointed Man*, Barbellion surmised that the reader who recommended the book had been 'combed out' and replaced by a godly man, solicitous for the firm's reputation as a publisher of schoolbooks and bibles. 'My malignant fate has not forsaken me.' A year later Frank Swinnerton took the book on, and Barbellion urged his brother, whose wife was pregnant: 'If it's a boy, call him Andrew Chatto Windus. Then perhaps the firm will give him a royalty when he is published at the Font.' When would the book come out? He was dying, but 'I'm digging my heels in awaiting those two old tortoises, Chatto and Windus'. The book arrived the next morning: 'the sun is shining'. Barbellion had tried for the 'candour and verisimilitude' he admired in Joyce's *Portrait of the Artist*, but it was no use. Chatto had cut out 'two splendid entries about prostitutes and other stuff'. The book wouldn't leave his widow a rich woman.

One of the ideas for unwritten stories proposed by Samuel Butler stars a free-thinking father who has an illegitimate son (which he considers the proper thing). Then the son takes to immoral ways. He turns Christian, joins the clergy, and insists on marrying.

It is an ancient belief, or assumption, that a genuine, serious writer shocks the public; he lives in a permanent mode of oppugnancy, at war with the prime dogmas of the status quo.

Latterly that noble stance or ambition is losing its substance. Nowadays the serious writer will, as ever, decline to meet expectations – he is still a rebel, and oppugnancy endures, but by seeking *not* to shock the public. Or, that is, he will shock them by not shocking them. The public may not appreciate this very much.

Somebody said recently, 'As a writer, I want to make people look at things they don't want to.' His book has headed the bestseller list for six months running. 'Know that our great showmen/Are those who show what we want to have shown': thus Brecht ('Deliver the Goods'). Our great shockmen are those who shock us as we want to be shocked.

Liber Amoris (1823), a high-falutin, highly inaccurate or crudely ironic title: the subtitle, 'The New Pygmalion', the best thing around. (Compare 'The Modern Prometheus', subtitle of *Frankenstein*, five years earlier.) The torments and ignominies of adolescent infatuation, yes, one understands all that, even though a little later it grows incomprehensible. But Hazlitt was forty-two, and (which may be beside the point) had been married for twelve years, when he met Sarah Walker, his landlady's daughter. Something of a tease, Sarah, with the uneasily self-righteous, pathetically defensive air of her station in life: 'I am but a tradesman's daughter', and the gratification of getting her own back on the clever-clever gentry. Clearly no 'angel from Heaven', and not exactly 'a practised, callous jilt, a regular lodging-house decoy' either. Certainly not a patch on Richardson's adroit and pertinacious Pamela (subtitled 'Virtue Rewarded'), but more authentic, I'd say, truer to ordinary life.

How could Hazlitt bring himself to set down and (albeit anonymously) publish such a frightful mishmash of mawkishness, hurt pride, abjectness, nagging lust and spite, almost as if he were a contemporary of ours? Did he think it would shock? (So unmanly, and Hazlitt the famously 'manly' writer!) Because frankness is a virtue, and cannot be exercised too often? Because the story demonstrates how carnal desire can interfere with a great literary and philosophical mind? (Or the other way about.) As 'a document in madness' (a *fin de siècle* view)? Or (a modern view) because Hazlitt was attempting – no doubt a commendable aim – to 'reach a democratic erotic moment'?

'There is an unseemly exposure of the mind, as well as of the body': Hazlitt, 'On Disagreeable People', 1827. I wish I hadn't read the book. Or that I had read it in what is considered the proper way of reading – without feeling anything in particular.

A new novel, Anne Haverty's *The Far Side of a Kiss* (a subtitle might have come in handy), tells the story from Sarah Walker's point of view: 'He has put me in a book. He had but a frail steel nib for his weapon but he has destroyed me by it.' As well as stabbing himself in the foot. Ungrateful young madam, one is tempted to exclaim, considering he made her a celebrity. But what damage they could do in their day, when not everyone yearned to join the celebrito-cracy, those frail steel nibs.

A lengthy letter arrives from the Vice-Chancellor of Cambridge University, urging me to consider making a gift to the Cantab Fund, and wanting to share with me his thoughts about Cambridge. He is still pleased to say he studied there, and he feels an instant rapport whenever he meets a fellow graduate. Supporting the Fund with a personal gift is his way of repaying a debt. 'You alone can quantify the value of your Cambridge education', but a typical donation of £500 plus reclaimed tax will amount to ... The Vice-Chancellor says I shall shortly receive a telephone call from a current student who will ask for my response to the present letter.

Ten days later I receive a call from a current student. The conversation goes like this. I ask whether he knows anything about me:

– Well, he knows my name, address and telephone number, and year of matriculation.

– Nothing else?

– He gathers I am a freelance writer.

– Good, but I advise him not to become a freelance writer.

– Oh no, no chance of that, he's an economist.

– Doesn't he feel that this arm-twisting is a shabby trick, unworthy of the great institution in question? How could he lend himself to it?

– He says: 'We are paid.'

An utterly disarming reply. Any method of making money is good. Money launders itself. I make my excuses and put the phone down.

Would you believe it? (Why not?) Four days later a similar letter arrives from the Master of Downing College. Like Cambridge University, Downing College is a great success, but being successful costs money. The Master reveals that 'a bright and intelligent Downing student', he or she, will contact me by phone and ask me to consider making a gift of £25 per month through a five-year deed of covenant which, plus reclaimed tax, will yield ... Happily you can tick a box on an enclosed card if you don't wish to be phoned.

Also enclosed is a brochure drawing attention to Downing celebrities, a mixed bunch including Trevor Nunn, John Cleese, Michael Winner, Mike Atherton, F. W. Maitland and F. R. Leavis. I have an uncomfortable feeling that the proceeds of an earlier appeal to which I contributed were spent on a new boathouse.

No book about China, however slim or rudimentary, fails to mention Sima Qian (Ssu-ma Ch'ien), early first-century BC moralist, prose stylist and official court historian. While engaged on his much admired *Historical Records* he fell foul of the Emperor for defending a friend, a defeated general, who had been unjustly punished. Sima

Qian was sentenced to death, but chose castration – a fate considered worse than death – since this allowed him to finish his monumental work. A scholar and a gentleman, and a true writer.

Books have their fates. Quite recently offers to schools of free sets of the Everyman Library were rejected on the grounds that there wasn't room for them, and anyway they were not 'relevant'. It appears that some of us – once you would have said the least expected of us – have the strange ambition to start all over afresh. In 213 BC the then Emperor of China, desiring to wipe out history and establish himself as the First Emperor, ordered all books to be destroyed except for those on 'relevant' subjects such as medicine and agriculture. Scholars who resisted the edict were burnt together with the books. The idea was 'to make the people ignorant' (and therefore respectful) and prevent 'the use of the past to discredit the present' (for example by suggesting that the present Emperor wasn't really unique). However, books have a way of returning from the dead, of popping up in time's backlist. Sufficient documents survived for Sima Qian to record the doings and the death of the 'immortal' First Emperor.

At first Dorothea Brooke found Mr Casaubon 'as instructive as Milton's "affable archangel" '. (A master of exposition, Raphael was instructive at considerable length – 'affable' comes from the Latin 'speak' – and admonitory to little purpose.) Mr Casaubon's 'Key to all Mythologies', had it lived up to its name, would have opened some interesting doors.

A poor student passed the Chinese Imperial Examinations with flying colours, and was to receive his due reward from the Emperor himself. Alas, he was so unprepossessing that the Emperor declined to meet him. In despair, he threw himself into the sea. A kindly aquatic dragon took pity on him and bore him up to heaven. Set among the stars, he was appointed the God of Literature.

*

Always captivating, the irruption into fantasy of the strictly reasonable and realistic. Haitian zombies clump heavily along, performing menial tasks for unscrupulous plantation owners, whereas in Chinese accounts reanimated corpses proceed in a series of little hops. Well, they would, wouldn't they? Rigor mortis prevents them from bending their limbs. Comparable arguments for inducing much-needed credibility are found throughout society, especially among the ruling classes.

Italo Svevo has noted Proust's perfect vision of reality: 'And when this reality of his becomes satire, it becomes so almost without his intervention. Reality can sometimes make itself heard solely through precision.' That's the way to do it. Let things speak for themselves. (With just a little help: see Swift and his *Modest Proposal*.) Yet some things, no matter how actual, defy our sense of reality, defy satire. What to do then? Apart from ranting and raving and gnashing of teeth, ambitious to emulate Pope, but stuck with Sporus's 'florid impotence', frothing at the mouth, a surly, superannuated, senile mouth. When it seems most difficult not to write satire, it can prove impossible to write it.

Postmodernism defines itself, enacts its (absence of) meaning. You hardly understand that you don't understand it. In other matters one understands fairly precisely what one doesn't understand, and perhaps one tries to understand (and possibly succeeds at times). But here one does not understand even that. One isn't really meant to. This, if I understand correctly (which I probably do not), has to do with the presence of relativities: i.e. the absence of absolutes. One cannot conceive clearly of relativities because one cannot visualize them clearly; they are all equally cogent or not, determinedly indeterminate, and innumerable in number. In the past you may have distrusted absolutes, and broken the rules that attend them. But they remained there, absolutes and rules, they didn't suddenly drop out of sight. They, and the departing and deviating from them, gave meaning to you and your actions. Postmodernism is the evacuation of absolutes and – not the loss (which would be noticed) – the non-existence of meaning. Naturally it is not as simple as this sounds. If it were, you might understand it, and then it wouldn't be what it is.

Perhaps one thing one might come to conjecture is that postmodernism is distinctly premodern, not to say primeval, and associated with the turgid pre-academic soup (unhurried matrix of the brain), before thought came into the world, the long, dark ages of relatively blissful un-understanding, when life was grounded in a scattering of simple relativities: hot, cold, empty, full, pleasing, displeasing. Sophisticated persons love to play at the primitive, fancying themselves as First Emperor of some pristine dominion of organized entropy, expunging the past, breaking images when to do so brings plaudits rather than persecution. (Paul Hoggart, television critic, has observed that 'Iconoclasm is our most popular spectator sport'), dipping their toes in moral vacuity while keeping handy the telephone number of the nearest police station. Impossible though it be to understand postmodernism, it is not hard to understand postmodernists.

A character in John Lanchester's *The Debt to Pleasure*, pressed by the narrator to provide a distinction between modernism and postmodernism, proposes that 'Modernism is about finding out how much you could get away with leaving out. Postmodernism is about how much you can get away with putting in.' Something so comprehensible, so sweetly reasonable, deserves to be true.

A man of his time and equally of ours, Montaigne wrote: 'When you hear such grammatical terms as metonymy, metaphor and allegory, they seem to signify some rare, strange tongue, don't they? Yet they are concepts that bear on the prattling of your chambermaid' ('On the vanity of words').

'I like making puns myself,' confessed Margaret Drabble in a radio talk back in the 1970s, 'but some of them are so obscure that nobody ever notices them.' Her favourite pun among her own occurs when one of her characters – he is left-handed – describes his skill at card tricks as 'a sinister dexterity'. No one else, she added, had admired the pun.

No doubt I have mentioned elsewhere my favourite home-made pun. When Faust is lamenting the disappearance of his paramour, Helen (lately of Troy), Mephistopheles suggests, with the flippancy he deploys to belittle human ambitions and emotions, that she has gone to Paris for the weekend. So?: (a) fashionable ladies like to take a short break in the French centre of fashion; or (b) if the putative reader is informed in Greek legend, Helen is visiting her former lover, Prince Paris. Easy, I'd think, not to notice any pun. To the best of my knowledge, only one reader spotted the two meanings – a Germanist – and he recoiled in horror. Still, the worst puns are often the best.

When the headmistress in Winifred Holtby's novel, *South Riding*, declared, 'I was born to be a spinster, and by God, I'm going to spin', no doubt every reader caught on and, far from taking offence, smiled appreciatively.

A friend tells me of a double pun that pleased him. He was present at a wedding when for some reason the proceedings were held up, and he remarked brightly, 'Ah, a technical hitch.' The bridegroom taught at a technical college. It's to be hoped that this pleasantry eased the embarrassment, and bride and groom got successfully hitched.

Permanent Secretary Tuzzi, in Musil's *The Man Without Qualities*, held that while one couldn't quite manage without them in witty conversation, puns should never be too good, because that was middle-class.

Apparently unaware of a convoluted incident recorded in *The Golden Legend*, Christina Rossetti wondered that the association of fire with St Blaise had not been accounted for. A pun on his name had been suggested as the link, but at least 'one author of repute' had branded this as absurd. 'Yet let us hope,' she wrote, 'that this particular pun if baseless is also blameless.' Mind you, 'puns and such like are a frivolous crew likely to misbehave unless kept within strict bounds'. St Paul came out strongly against 'foolish talking and jesting, which are not convenient' (unlike a straightforward 'giving of thanks'). Thus the entry in *Time Flies: A Reading Diary* for 3 February 1885. All the same, in the entry for 13 March, Christina Rossetti said she felt 'neither excited nor helped to observe Lent' by being referred to the German root of the word. It was a false etymology – or a pun – that came to her aid, linking the word with 'loan': 'that which is lent' rather than 'bestowed', 'forty chances to be used or abused', and so forth.

Christina Rossetti had a more robust sense of humour than she is commonly credited (or discredited) with. On 13 February she declared that tact is a gift and 'likewise a grace'. True, tact has a weak side: its love of conciliation and dislike of quarrelling may 'incline it to overstep the boundary of truth' or distort it. Yet the daily, practical value of tact can scarcely be exaggerated. This she illustrated with a far-fetched, hardly 'daily' tale of a certain man who was challenged to fight a duel, and consequently was entitled to choose the weapon. 'Javelins,' he announced. But whoever had heard of such a weapon in this connection? 'Well, that is mine.' And the duel never came off.

'Pornography is a highly emotive word, but it's all in the eye of the beholder': thus the editor of *Desire Direct*, an introductions magazine on the Internet. Highly emotive indeed: prostitutes plus writing. It has been complained that the Obscene Publications Act of 1959 offers no definition of 'deprave and corrupt'. True, some words are difficult to define at all effectively by means of other words. Thesauruses just don't help. For example, Please define the following: 'pervert' and 'degrade', 'debauch' and 'debase', 'corrupt' and 'deprave'. Every definition involves us in further definitions. This happens whenever common sense, the eye of the beholder, the ear of the listener, have been ousted.

Back in the early 1970s I wrote in an account of childhood and growing up that after the main entry in Latin and Greek ('pulmonary neoplasm'), my father's death certificate read 'Contributory Cause of Death: Septic Teeth'. I may have glimpsed those words in 1934, before the certificate was hidden away, but how could I have remembered them? Probably made it all up, oh dear. Now my sister has unearthed the document, and reads it to me over the phone. I had got it absolutely right. There's something rather reassuring about that. Also the reverse: these days I would have forgotten the wording of my own certificate forty-eight hours after it was made out.

This notebook ('Feint' and 'Discontinued') has a marbled cover; it looks dusty even if it isn't; it probably is. Never before have I gone so long without writing anything. (Or being asked to write something.) Most depressing. Can always read, of course, but that may be mortifying. Some people don't go long without writing a lot.

In a flash of the melodrama that quite often lightens the surrounding gloom, I have a vision of a decent fellow in a novel of yesteryear, sunk in disgrace or despair, putting a gun to his head or in his mouth. I look around my desk. Nothing like a gun in sight. Nearest thing is a cylinder of lighter gas. It's rich in sensational reading matter. 'No smoking.' 'Take precautionary measures against static discharges.' And 'Deliberately inhaling the contents may be harmful or even fatal.' Only *even* fatal? I wouldn't want to do myself mere harm. I fill my lighter obediently, take up my pipe ('Wait one minute before using lighter. Ignite lighter away from face'), and compose myself to jot down these small happenings.

Or put it this way. The ageing scribbler feels glum. He tells himself: Your *raison d'être* has disappeared. But then, it occurs to him, his *être* is about to disappear. This cheers him up, briefly.

Latterly the terms senility and dementia have yielded to Alzheimer's disease – though Alois Alzheimer first described the disease as far back as 1906. A more scientific term, one supposes, free of tendentious secular associations. But was it, with its vague approximate suggestions of old and home, old home, home for the old, just a little euphemistic or softened in its beginnings? Not any longer, now that it's on everyone's lips, even those normally shy of foreign names. In this field, euphemisms soon mutate. Our preoccupation with matters of health and ill health is narcissistic and debilitating. Without it – on television, hospitals compete with kitchens for first place – we might be healthier and we would be happier (for a while). Last things are best left until last, or last but one.

In age there is an insidious temptation to write about age, its discontents and its dark comedies. Old people don't much care to hear about this, they know the discontents (and if they're lucky they know the comedies), but are usually happy to share their experiences with other old people. As for the young, age is a foreign country, its denizens mumbling treasonably in a foreign tongue. 'Growing old is, of course, a crime of which we grow more guilty every day': Penelope Fitzgerald, in 'The Axe', 1975.

I notice a large, fading notice on the wall of the local church, which stands at a busy crossroads:

BEFORE   MAKE
ENTERING   SURE OF
BOX   YOUR EXIT

Very civic-minded of the church to dispense traffic advice. But there's no box junction in sight. Then, when I'm halfway across the busy road, I make out a dim shape in the centre of the notice: a crude representation of a coffin. Ah, a religious message, that's more like it! A motorist toots at me: 'Want to get yourself killed?'

The story about firing squads has it that one of the rifles contained a blank cartridge, so that every member of the squad could tell himself, it wasn't me who killed the poor sod. (Compare the less happy hangman and headsman.)

In the world of medicine, 'healthcare', the patient passes from one specialist to another, one surgeon to another, one nurse to another. Some of them must be firing blanks. So who is really responsible for you? God is. Groan.

'I should not really object to dying if it were not followed by death': Thomas Nagel, *Mortal Questions*. Others might not really object to death if it were not preceded by dying.

Am taken with a story told by Jane Austen's nephew. She didn't wish her 'occupation' to be known or suspected by servants or visitors, and therefore wrote on small sheets of paper which could readily be hidden under a piece of blotting-paper. 'There was, between the front door and the offices, a swing-door which creaked when it was opened, but she objected to having this little inconvenience remedied, because it gave her notice when anyone was coming.' That's about as far as biographies of writers need go. I came across it in Claire Tomalin's biography of Jane Austen.

At the age of forty-one, Jane Austen acknowledged that 'Sickness is a dangerous indulgence at my time of life.' She died a few months later. On occasion illness, if not of the terminal kind, has been reckoned a blessing in disguise. Commenting on the infidelities of authors, Margaret Oliphant observed that Thomas Carlyle appeared to have 'trodden the straight way'. To which Jane Carlyle replied: 'My dear, if Mr Carlyle's digestion had been better there is no telling what he might not have done!'

Things have come to a sorry pass when one puzzles over the language of junk mail. An Indian take-away in Wimbledon, 'climbing new heights', offers 'the same authenticity of the much relished "Indian cuisine" of the Moghul days', and informs us that it 'has been gloved in a high-tech interior and geared towards the future'. What if you want it now?

Increasingly, mail – not only junk – comes addressed to a Mr or Mrs Enri. Computers dock your name to suit their miserable high-tech convenience. Soon we shall all be reduced to numbers – the digital revolution.

A support group has been formed in America to help 'innocent good women who have been heckled, ridiculed, shamed and maimed because they have the name Monica', and to celebrate the reputations that many earlier Monicas have enjoyed. The name – no jokes about monikers, please – is said by some to derive from Latin *monēre*, to warn, counsel, admonish. For me it means – and will always mean, no matter how many Lewinskys hit the headlines – the mother of St Augustine. Her son confessed that she suffered greater pangs during his spiritual pregnancy than when giving birth to him in the flesh.

'ROMEO SEEKS JULIET. Slim man, aged 37, university-educated, with boyish looks, seeks the company of sincere lady, 25–50, for loving relationship.' 'MR DARCY SEEKS ELIZABETH. Jut-jawed, jodphurs [*sic*]-wearing, tall male, 40, seeks warm, winsome, witty, worshipable female, for reciprocally rapturous romance.

Lake-loving lass only, please': Personals, *Independent on Sunday*. How good to see that literature remains a living force.

Reality, having travestied itself, has made hay of satire. A document comes my way which defies classification. Headed 'GOD'S TOTAL QUALITY MANAGEMENT QUESTIONNAIRE', the document states that 'God would like to thank you for your belief and patronage' and 'in order to better serve your needs, God asks that you take a few minutes to answer the following questions'. Responses will be kept confidential, and you need not disclose your name or address, unless of course you wish for direct feedback.

'How did you find out about your deity?: Newspaper, Bible, Torah, Television, Divine Inspiration, Dead Sea Scrolls, My Mamma Done Tol' Me, Near Death Experience, Near Life Experience, Burning Shrubbery, Other Ways (please specify).'

'Did your God come to you undamaged, with all parts in good working order and with no obvious breakage or missing attributes? If no, please describe the problems you initially encountered: Not eternal, Finite in space, Does not occupy or inhabit the entire cosmos, Not omniscient, Not omnipotent, Permits sex outside of marriage, Prohibits sex outside of marriage, Makes or permits bad things to happen to good people, When beseeched, does not stay beseeched, Requires burnt offerings, Requires virgin sacrifices, etc.'

'What factors were relevant in your decision to acquire a deity?: Indoctrinated by parents, Needed a reason to live, Needed focus whom to despise, Hate to think for myself, Fear of death, Wanted to piss off parents, Needed a day away from work, My shrubbery caught fire and a loud voice commanded me to do it, etc.'

'Are you currently using any other source of inspiration in addition to God: Tarot, Lottery, Astrology, Television, Fortune cookies, *Playboy* and/or *Playgirl*, Sex, Drugs, Rock and roll, Alcohol, Tea leaves, The Internet, Burning shrubbery, Teletubbies, etc.?'

'God employs a limited degree of Divine Intervention to preserve the balanced level of felt presence and blind Faith. Which would you prefer?: More Divine Intervention, Less Divine Intervention, Current degree of Divine Intervention is just about right.'

'Do you have any additional comments or suggestions for improving the quality of God's services? Attach an additional sheet if necessary.'

'As an incentive (the flesh is agreed to be weak), it is promised that if you return the completed questionnaire by a certain date you will be entered in a draw for the One Free Miracle of Your Choice.'

The document concludes: 'Thank you, (signed) Daryl, Clerk of the Supreme Being of the Apocalypse.'

The demotic language may give us to pause, yet there is no sound reason to suppose that God is a snob. Many of the issues broached are of crucial importance to us all in both theory and practice. Some of the marginal allusions I have omitted, for instance, pop stars, talk-show presenters, sporting personages, models and role models, cooks and comics, and other celebrities unknown to me. More often than not, God is considered omniscient (if at times pretending not to be), and is clearly no shrinking violet, but one might expect there to be certain topics, trivial, vulgar or otherwise inappropriate, which neither he nor his agents, nor even self-appointed evangelists, would dream of pondering in public. But then, can we be sure? He moves in a mysterious way.

Here's something of a wonder performed. 'If the clerk to the journals of the House of Lords should die, I had some hopes that my kinsman, who had the place at his disposal, would appoint me to succeed him.' When William Cowper mentioned this to a friend, they 'both expressed an earnest wish for his death, that I might be provided for'. The occupant of the coveted position promptly died. And the consequent sense of God's wrath, along with some doubt as to God's existence, unfitted Cowper, then in his early thirties, for any place at all. He repeatedly made to end his life by drinking a phial of laudanum, but some invisible hand forced the bottle away. He took his penknife into bed, placed it beneath his left breast, and leant his full weight on it: the point broke off. He tried to hang himself with his garter, but it slipped off the bedpost. He climbed on a chair and looped the garter over a half-opened door: the garter snapped. He had done his best, and failed. God had cast him out. When Jesus cursed the barren fig tree, it was Cowper he had in mind. (This might throw light on a perplexing parable.) If Cowper went into the street, 'I thought the people stood and laughed at me, and held me in contempt.' He bought a ballad from one who was singing it in the street, 'because I thought it was written on me'.

Thus poor Cowper and his 'quivering sensibility': a 'stricken deer', a timorous, melancholic, ineffectual wreck, not merely damned but 'damned below Judas'. And yet, what a powerful ego: he couldn't hear a street ballad without supposing himself the subject of it. What a towering awareness of self: *me*, 'Me miserable! how could I escape/ Infinite wrath and infinite despair!' Admittedly the castaway, swept overboard, did drown; but Cowper perished 'beneath a rougher sea/And whelm'd in deeper gulfs than he'.

It's not so surprising that someone of such intensities, with such a command of metaphor, should be capable, in a calmer state of mind, of near-Popeian satire, and of some notably humane poems, cogent and idiosyncratic. 'The Negro's Complaint': 'Prove that you have human feelings,/ Ere you proudly question ours!' And on that old and ever new argument, that if, say, we don't sell arms, someone else will:

> If foreigners likewise would give up the trade,
> Much more on behalf of your wish might be said;
> But while they get riches by purchasing blacks,
> Pray tell me why we may not also go smacks?

And on hunting: 'Detested sport,/ That owes its pleasures to another's pain.'

Cowper was quite a tough customer, after all. 'I was a grovelling creature once', but behind a frowning providence, God hides a smiling face. He knew what he was about. 'God is his own interpreter,/And he will make it plain.' Interpretation can take time, of course.

Michael Hamburger translates Ernst Jandl's *'nichts und etwas'* ('nothing and something'):

> nothing in my head
> I sit down
> at the typewriter
> insert a sheet
> with nothing on it
>
> with something on it
> I extract the sheet
> from the typewriter
> and read as a text
> something out of my head.

Small to the point of minimal, yet the poem 'celebrates a miracle and mystery of sorts', Hamburger comments. 'Something has really come out of nothing.' Yes, the miracle and mystery some of us have relied on. But when there's nothing available in the head, when the head is stuffed with incipiences, banal foibles, petty grievances and caprices? Gone, it seems, are the days when poetry warned and exhorted, desolated and consoled. Nowadays its ambition is to amuse or intrigue fleetingly: a very minor branch of the entertainment industry, less imagination than fancy, less fancy than whimsy. Czeslaw Milosz has asked why we feel shame when looking through a book of poems, as if the author, for some unknown reason, is addressing the worse side of our nature. 'Seasoned with jokes, clowning, satire,/Poetry still knows how to please./ . . . But the grave combats where life is at stake/ Are fought in prose.' Not that I have anything against entertainment that entertains rather than panders to its audience. And there's decent sense in Kit Wright's foray against pomposity and empty earnestness: ' . . . unacknowledged legislators!/ How's that for insane afflatus?'

'The greatness of poets lies in grasping with their words what they only glimpse with their minds': Paul Valéry. Is the greatness of prose writers really any different?

'Here is a marvel: we now have many more poets than judges and connoisseurs of poetry. Poetry is easier to write than to appreciate': Montaigne. Some things don't change: a chastening thought, but also – one comes to see – a cheering thought.

Since much of the poetry written today might just as well – or rather better – be written as prose, I have decided (with some help from outside) to confine myself to writing prose. Even so, reading is another matter.

Laugh at yourself in private by all means (means won't be hard to come by), but go easy in public. Anyone seen laughing at himself is truly laughable. Coleridge tells two apposite stories. A certain Nehemiah Higginbottom published a satirical sonnet about the house that Jack built, demonstrating the indiscriminate use of ornate, overblown language and imagery ('And this reft house is that, the which he built'), and incorporating phrases stolen from Coleridge's poems. This was believed to have wounded Coleridge sorely. It happened that he was himself the author of it. And then he was seen as the unhappy victim of a cruel epigram directed against 'The Ancient Mariner', already an object of derision:

> Your poem must eternal be,
> Dear sir! it cannot fail.
> For 'tis incomprehensible,
> And without head or tail!

something he had composed and printed in *The Morning Post.*

Asking for trouble ... And yet there may be occasions, rather rare, when a person can feel decently (or superstitiously) obliged to do in public what he more commonly does in private.

In his prose Coleridge wanders off at all angles and in a number of tongues, and the drift of his announced theme is hard to keep in view. The asides are often the best, most comprehensible things there. In his obscure meditations on the distinction between fancy and imagination, he remarks that 'in all societies there exists an instinct of growth, a certain collective, unconscious good sense working progressively to desynonymize those words originally of the same meaning'. A large, learned book condensed in a short limpid sentence! Elsewhere, in the course of a lengthy and elaborate diatribe against a now forgotten blood-and-thunder, Charles Robert Maturin's play, *Bertram, or The Castle of St Aldobran*, and within an aside on the English origin of the German drama (flattering neither nation), there comes a further aside characterizing James Hervey's equally forgotten *Meditations among the Tombs*, which is 'poetic only on account of its utter unfitness for prose, and might as appropriately be called prosaic from its utter unfitness for poetry'.

'He would have done better if he had known less' (Hazlitt). Or remembered less or been less enthusiastically digressive, less ready to invoke his sprawling knowledge at every opportunity whether pertinent or not, and if he had moderated his meanderings, what a terrific critic he would have been! In fact he often is. And perhaps without those monstrous contexts there would be no precious asides.

A splendid instance of accuracy, succinctness, force and general application arises in Coleridge's *Notebooks*, apropos of the demands Milton makes on the reader. The latter is 'surrounded with sense; it rises in every line', 'there are no lazy intervals': 'If this be called obscurity, let it be remembered that it is such an obscurity as is a compliment to the reader; not that vicious obscurity, which proceeds from a muddled head.'

Goethe's saying both fascinates and discomposes: 'If in old age intelligent and thoughtful persons set little store by knowledge, it is only because they have asked too much of it and of themselves.' In what way have they asked too much? Did they expect that knowledge would fend off age? Or preserve their health? Or keep their memory – without which knowledge deserts us – in good repair? Not if they were intelligent and thoughtful. Have they worn themselves out in the acquiring of knowledge (and we have it on good authority that those who increase knowledge increase sorrow)? Are they, when they cease to prize knowledge, still intelligent and thoughtful, or is that asking too much of them? Or has some different, darker knowledge taken them over? A sense of the absurd, say. 'We are tiny specks in the infinite vastness of the universe; our lives are mere instants, . . . we will all be dead any minute,' as Thomas Nagel puts it. And 'In ordinary life a situation is absurd when it includes a conspicuous discrepancy between pretension or aspiration and reality.' (But note Pascal: the eternal silence of those infinite spaces terrified him, yet 'Through space the universe encloses me and swallows me up like a speck; through thought I enclose it.')

Nagel concludes with words that some may find faintly comforting: 'If *sub specie aeternitatis* there is no reason to believe that anything matters, then that does not matter either, and we can approach our absurd lives with irony instead of heroism or despair.' Irony can stand a lot of weight, but not that much. The modern concept of the absurd, while it carries some respectable character references, is distinctly unGoethean. Four years after his reflection on old age's disappointment with knowledge, when he was seventy-six, Goethe proposed that growing older meant entering on a new business in changed circumstances, 'and one must either give up activity altogether or assume the new role with awareness and intention'. This leaves questions unanswered, but that's in the nature of wise sayings, and of life with its propensity to raise new questions.

Mixed blessings. The statement that falling out of bed kills more people than the human form of BSE is meant to reassure, but at the expense of our night-life. There are questions best left unanswered, or unasked. 'Lord, let me know mine end, and the number of my days.' A gentleman of seventy-two years reports that when he went for his annual flu jab, he was offered one for pneumonia as well. This being new to him, he asked when he would need another jab. The nurse told him, 'Oh, you won't. They last about ten years.'

*

> Then lo! the sainted MONITOR is born,
> Whose pious face some sacred texts adorn,
> As artful sinners cloak the secret sin,
> To veil with seeming grace the guile within:
> So moral Essays on his front appear,
> But all is carnal business in the rear.

'Carnal business in the rear' may bring Proust's M. de Charlus to mind, but these lines on the Sunday newspapers were written in 1785 by George Crabbe. In his different idiom and availing himself of satirist's licence, Karl Kraus touched on the theme in 1911, submitting that the contraceptive ads were the only decent, sensible and tasteful contributions appearing in the Viennese papers, until the press spoilt it all by repudiating on the highly moral front pages what it promoted against payment on the back pages.

Things don't change; our perception of them often does. 'There is nothing either good or bad, but thinking makes it so': a relativist slogan, not Shakespearian wisdom, merely Hamlet's polite way of disagreeing with Rosencrantz and Guildenstern. Here is Baudelaire in *Mon coeur mis à nu*, 1863: 'Every newspaper, from the first line to the last, is nothing but a web of horrors. War, crime, rapine, shamelessness, torture, the crimes of princes, the crimes of nations, the crimes of individuals, a delirium of universal atrocity. And it is with this revolting aperitif that the civilized man starts his morning meal every day. Everything, in this world, reeks of crime: the paper, the walls and the face of man. I cannot comprehend how clean hands could touch a newspaper without a convulsion of disgust.' Compare this with a congratulatory headline in *The Times*, 8 March 2002: 'We're a nation of newspaper addicts.'

'Those who ne'er deigned their Bible to peruse/ Would think it hard to be denied their News,' wrote Crabbe, 'And such this mental food, as we may call/ Something to all men, and to some men all.' Enough to poison our minds. How much longer, as communications proliferate and our resistance weakens further, can we rely on what Wordsworth in his reflections on the 'degrading thirst after outrageous stimulation' identified as 'certain inherent and indestructible qualities of the human mind'? (To begin with, 'certain' often insinuates a degree of uncertainty.)

At least I have cancelled the Sunday paper, much to that day's advantage.

Dozing off, I remember a childhood accident on my bike, speeding downhill against traffic lights, when the brakes had failed. I was lucky. And now I think of a young granddaughter, an intrepid cyclist. Next I see a child on a bike approaching a lamppost at speed, thudding into it – and being catapulted to the top of the lamppost, where she (rather than he) performs a triumphant comic dance. A last-ditch effort of will there, and I jerk awake. A few moments later, reverie would have drifted into dream, and a far less cheerful outcome.

No letters for a whole week. (Not counting charities, that is, and offers to release cash tied up in my property on the tacit assumption that in return I shall die before long.) What does this mean? Perhaps it means that I haven't written any letters for a month.

For lack of anything better to do, I copy-edit a book published earlier in the year, a rather good book by an American professor of English. But oh dear – 'obselete', 'wimper', 'Scandanavian', 'Cartusian', 'Huysman'. And tut, tut – an extended family produces lots of cousins 'for my sister, my brother, and I'. I think passingly of billing the publisher.

Some poor devil had come to think of himself as a book. More tattered every year, he had to admit, jacket torn, spine creaking, dried up and yellowing inside. Sad, but only to be expected. At least no one had burnt or pulped him. One day it struck him that he was going out of print, and certainly wouldn't be reissued. Ah well, that too was in the nature of things; and just possibly he would live on residually, in a few libraries, on a few private shelves. For a while. All paper is flesh and one book drives out another.

Kafka was less literal (so to speak), but more insistent in his outcry: it wasn't that he had what is called a flair for writing or a way with words; rather, 'I am made of literature, I am nothing else, and cannot be anything else.'

'You're mentioned in this book,' I told Claire (granddaughter and intrepid cyclist, then aged six and three-quarter years), showing a copy of *Play Resumed*. She looked herself up in the index – she knows her way about books – and leafed through to page 8. Didn't seem thrilled by what she read. 'You've been immortalized,' I quipped feebly, inviting trouble. 'But who'll buy the book?' she asked.

*

In Mandarin, I gather, the film *The Full Monty* carries the title 'Six Naked Pigs'. Not inevitably a gross slur, given the Chinese fondness for pork. Peter Farb (*Word Play*, 1974) has pointed out that when Charlie Chan, Earl Derr Biggers's Chinese-Hawaiian detective, says 'Honourable inspector is welcome to humble abode', the 'subtle suggestion of esteem' in the Chinese form – conveyed by the specific grammar used – has been converted into 'unsubtle' (i.e. clunking) words such as 'honourable' and 'humble'. (Still, Chan had to speak English if the books were to sell. And one wonders just how subtle in suggestion the Chinese locutions remain after centuries of use.) When Chan addresses an arrogant, racist Bostonian: 'Humbly asking pardon to mention it, I detect in your eyes slight flame of hostility. Quench it, if you will be so kind' (*The House Without a Key*, 1925), for all I can tell he has contrived a pretty effective way, both imploring and (more tellingly) deploring, of blending Oriental honorifics and dishonorifics in makeshift English. Those who are addressed in pidgin often come off better than those speaking it to them. A Chinese notable (Chiang Kai-shek, Sun Yat-sen?) was asked by his well-meaning British neighbour at a formal dinner: 'You likee soupee?' At the end of the meal, the Chinese gentleman stood up and delivered a speech in flawless English. As he resumed his seat, he murmured to his neighbour: 'You likee speechee?' A case of pidgin pitched against pidgin.

'If you wish to avoid suspicion, do not tie up your shoes in a melon field or adjust your hat under a plum tree.' This Chinese proverb cited by Claud Cockburn (*I, Claud . . .*) is couched in such exquisite English that its authenticity is called into question. You likee Chinese proverb?

According to a version of events given by Peter Farb, in July 1945 the Allies issued an ultimatum to Japan requiring the country to surrender, and the Japanese Prime Minister replied that his cabinet would *mokusatsu* the ultimatum, apparently meaning that it would 'consider' the matter. But the word has another, very different meaning – 'take no notice of' – and the translators at Japan's overseas broadcasting agency read it in that sense. Consequently atomic bombs were dropped on Hiroshima, 6 August 1945, and Nagasaki, 9 August.

Less fatefully, in January 1999, a local government officer in Washington explained that he would need to be niggardly in his dealings with a certain fund. A black aide stormed out, complaints flooded in, and the officer resigned. The word itself (but everything is relative, we hear) is beyond reproach, of Scandinavian origin and related to 'niggling'. It was later argued that, even so, the officer should be punished for failing to see that the word was easily confused with a certain other one. It seems unfair – if not especially rare – that someone should suffer from the ignorance of other people. And the black Mayor of Washington later gave the officer a different job. If you wish to avoid suspicion, do not stray outside Basic English.

In Sisson's amusing poem, 'The Mirabel Sea': 'I wept intransitively, there was no one/ Who could be the object of my tears.' (Idle tears, then?) Compare a malapropism in a letter in the *Sunday Times*, 1988, cited by R.W. Burchfield: 'One, a head of English, could not explain the function of an intransigent verb and advised me to "forget it".' In other poems of his, Sisson's shedding of tears tends to be both transitive and intransigent.

'Toilet Paper: 100 per cent Recycled.' – 'Ugh!' she cries in horror and disgust, and disbelief. 'But,' I start, and then realize what she's thinking.

All this technology around – and yet they can't get the perforations to match in two-ply toilet paper.

'Spending a penny' was always more than a euphemism. The expression came from the old public lavatories with their penny-in-the-slot locks. It continues domestically: Thames Water informs its customers that every flushing of the toilet costs a (new) penny.

Letters to the Editor. A woman complains that her word-processing software won't tolerate a sentence more than three lines long, no matter how clearly expressed and immaculately punctuated. It questions her grammar, obliges her to use bullet-points unnecessarily, and offers to help when it notices she is writing a personal letter. All too plainly it considers her ignorant and incompetent.

A man discovers that his new computer has a hyperactive asterisk. Whenever he leaves the room briefly, on his return he finds a page completely filled with asterisks. Computers are officious – they spent their early years in offices – but those asterisks suggest they may not be altogether lacking in delicacy and decorum.

My one and only relationship with a computer didn't last long. With undue frequency and relish, it reminded me that it was registered to an incomparably more imposing concern and hence (the implication was) used to better things. Several times it turned sinister, informing me that I was engaged in an (unspecified) illegal activity. Before long it would be commenting on my sweaty fingertips or bad breath. One of us had to go. I am not surprised to hear of an online centre to help those suffering from Net addiction, and also a guide to polite behaviour online. For instance, 'DON'T WRITE IN CAPITALS – it looks as if you are SHOUTING, which is rude.' Point taken, but don't shout at me, it's rude.

'My daughter's PC has been unable to load several programs and a window has appeared saying "The Aliens are coming". Is this a virus?' Dear reader, to be on the safe side the first thing you should do is look out of the window. In the event that you see something out of the ordinary, don't SHOUT at it.

Before its keyboard proved too much for arthritic fingers, I used an Olympia Splendid, a pernickety but reasonably well-behaved electronic typewriter. At least until the day it broke free from my control as I was striving to make a small correction on the page (a review of Richard Hoggart's *Between Two Worlds*). The platen suddenly whirled round, the paper shot upwards and then stopped, and these words rattled out at a speed well beyond me in my heyday, correctly spelt and perfectly spaced, though not by me: 'Let's get to know each other. I'm' – at this point I recovered my wits sufficiently to stop the machine by switching off the power. Now I wish I hadn't, I wish I'd had the courage to let the message run its course. 'I'm . . .' Or do I?

> *'Half Price Memory': PC ad*
> What do you want for half the price,
> Half the nasty, half the nice?
> At your age passion's best aborted,
> The full-strength fact can't be afforded.
> 'Was £99.99. Now £49.99',
> Joys indistinct, griefs anodyne.
> A temperate tear, a low-pitched laugh,
> Suffice to form the better half.
> Yet who can tell what you may access,
> Some small beauty spot, some large abscess?
> Let the trained conscience known to Nietzsche
> Be your memories' tender teacher,
> So they kiss you while they bite –
> Then you'll know the price is right.

Wittgenstein had what look like grave reservations about Shakespeare's —greatness. He could '*nie etwas mit ihm anfangen*': never get
t   o
grips with him. (Cf. Kraus, unable to think of anything to say about the Führer: '*Mir fällt zu Hitler nichts ein*', 1933.) 'It could be put like this too . . .' What is conspicuous (relatively speaking) in the little I have seen of Wittgenstein on the subject of Shakespeare is his unenthusiastic avoidance of comprehensible complaint, and a

37

scrupulous – or/and fastidious, courteous, diffident – hedging of barely implicit bets. George Steiner, who (tiptoeing on thin ice) seems to some extent ('And yet . . .') to share in this nagging discontent, hints at a possible reason for Wittgenstein's reservations: how confident was his English, and could he have been 'resorting, consciously or not, to the masterly Schlegel-Tieck versions so essential to the central European literacy of his upbringing'? But what reasons does Steiner have for his own misgivings?

You sometimes find in the highest circles what looks much like the hope 'for eminence from the heresies of paradox' (Samuel Johnson, also on Shakespeare) which is common among those in rather low circles who are 'able to add nothing to truth'.

Early years. That there was no incentive to think (indeed, there was a tacit resistance) acted as an incentive to think, the only one. Not always deeply, good heavens no!, or to much effect, or even sensibly (that least of all). But still . . .

Curious encomia in a publishing conglomerate's spring list: 'mundane and magical' (having it both ways), 'traumatic' (a mundanely magical word), 'stunning' (recurrent and irritating; books stun only by falling on your head), 'cruel wit' (you wouldn't want a book to be merely witty, or solely cruel), 'wickedly funny' (very popular, this playing off adverb against adjective; cf. a film review in *The Times*: 'viciously funny'), 'menacing' (pick up a book and you take your life in your hands: brave you!), 'compulsive' (a step up or down from 'compelling'), 'unputdownable' (readers are a weak-willed race), 'mesmerizing' (that explains a lot), 'subversive', even 'treacherous', 'irreverent' (alternatively 'irreverant'), 'perceptive' (suggesting there is little to be said about the book), and 'literate' (suggesting there is nothing at all to be said). To which one could add this more elaborate eulogy of *The Times* 'book of the week': 'Forget the graphic sex, this is an author with a deranged, subversive grip on literary form and an envious skill for describing harsh landscape sparingly and beautifully.' ('Envious': near enough is good enough; cf. a BBC newsreader describing the chaotic scene at a derailment as 'incredulous'.)

Back to the spring lists. In terminology more commonly met in the thriller section, we are told regarding a scholarly book that ' . . . the Native American languages were in some cases literally beaten into extinction by brutal teachers of English'. One item stands out: 'Fast and funny, gruesome and depraved, the serial-killer novel to end all serial-killer novels. Literally.' Literally, eh? That'll be the day.

More about this mighty intensifier. On the occasion of Murray Walker's retirement as Formula One television commentator, the sports diarist of *The Times*, Simon Barnes, recalled a favourite observation by the man whose verbal thrills and spills enlivened many an arid Grand (or Grorn) Prix: 'And THAT is the Achilles heel of the McLaren and it is LITERALLY the heel because it's the GEARBOX . . .'

I notice from a reprint of Alison Lurie's *Real People* that a reviewer in the *Times Literary Supplement* praised it on first publication because 'in the most literal sense, it defies criticism'. It most literally (an intensification of an intensifier, in that something is either literal or it is not) defies? No, it defies criticism, which is a figure of speech, so that's OK. Defying criticism makes the critic's task easier. (That *Real People* defies criticism, the reviewer continued, 'in itself, is a pleasure'.) Or, it makes the critic's task impossible, and he is obliged to return the review copy to the commissioning periodical, explaining that the book has literally defied him. Which is no pleasure.

I thought the book quite pleasurable, but I could still criticize it, for all its defiance. (For instance, the story is somewhat predictable, except – predictably? – it ends abruptly, without finishing, and needs to be four or five pages longer.) But I won't, since I'm not being paid to do so.

*

Then there is – surprisingly common – the dangling or unattached participle. Robert Burchfield cites Lord Belstead speaking of Lord Whitelaw on BBC Radio in January 1988: 'Being unique, I am not going in any way to imitate him', and Richard Ingrams in 1987 writing of the house in which he grew up: 'Now demolished, I can call it to mind in almost perfect detail.' (Lord Belstead 'did not intend to imply that he was himself unique', and 'obviously Mr Ingrams had not been demolished'.)

People look baffled should you draw their attention to a dangling participle, and slightly anxious, as though they had omitted to adjust their dress. When, stumblingly, you seek to explain matters, they grow ratty: the intention is plain enough, no one would ever suppose it meant what (or so you say, and who are you to say?) it may signify grammatically, what does grammar count for anyway?

Have just come across a splendid specimen in Barbara Skelton's *Weep No More*: 'Dining alone in Ajaccio, a cockroach actually ran across the plate.' That should cure us of dangling participles – if anything could.

There we can just about make out what is going on, even though, from what we know of her, Miss Skelton was less likely than a cockroach to be dining alone. More ambiguous is a news item arising from comments on organic food made by Sir John Krebs, head of the Food Standards Agency. Harry Hadaway of the Soil Association, the organization responsible for certifying organic food and farmers, responded thus: 'As a historic supporter of genetically modified foods we feel Sir John continues not to represent the wishes of the British consumer . . .' Likewise 'As an investor in one of Dresdner RCM's unit trusts, we are writing regarding a proposed change in Dresdner Bank AG's ownership.' To the mistrustful eye it might seem as though rejecting the most obviously sensible 'rules' of grammar helps to obfuscate dodgy issues.

It can be a question, not of mere ambiguity or obfuscation, but of downright misrepresentation. Reviewing two biographies of Primo

Levi (*Times Literary Supplement*, 21 June 2002), Clive James notes of the author of one of them that 'like many another in the new generation of serious literati he somehow dodged remedial English on the way to his honours degree'. The biographer reports that at school Levi had a friend named Giorgio: 'Phlegmatic, lazy, sensitive and generous, Levi called him "Giorgione" . . .' The context suggests that the adjectives apply to Giorgio, while the word order indicates that they apply to Levi. Also, apropos of Natalia Ginzburg, the biographer states: 'Born to an exemplary anti-Fascist family, her father was arrested in Turin in 1934.' 'Unless there were exemplary anti-Fascist families before the advent of Fascism,' James observes, 'it was she, and not her father, who was born to the exemplary anti-Fascist family.' Such defects are all the worse in that Levi, a master of Italian prose, had learned to write 'at a time when a mistake was a mistake and not a sign of free expression'.

As I am writing this down there comes a letter from a professional philosopher who claims that 'As one of the shamefully discarded OUP poets' – see later in this book – 'I thought you might be interested to learn of my enclosed tilt against that great literary institution: I have opened a shop-cum-gallery of Oxford shame, right under (and up) their noses at 12 Broad Street.'

High Street optician discovers cataract in one eye and glaucoma in both. Six months later, hospital ophthalmologist tells me that cataracts in both eyes are due to wear and tear, and there's nothing to be done about them, while the glaucoma doesn't exist. Apparently the device used by opticians looking for glaucoma – a puff of air in the eye – creates the pressure it is meant to detect. Another self-fulfilling prophecy. What interesting medical times we live in!

Nothing to be done . . . Someone says, you should tell them you're a writer, you need your eyes. (That would be asking for trouble: blind him for his bad verses.) Who doesn't need his or her eyes? If you want personal treatment (this person is a writer, or whatever) you should make a personal payment to a professional person who operates privately. Money talks, but 'wear and tear' is not in its vocabulary, and that private professional will listen respectfully.

There's a charity that runs a factory where blind people make bookmarks. Something striking, something fine about this, a noble irony. More refined than turning out white sticks or dark glasses. The bookmark keeps reminding you how lucky you are. Probably, as the young man at the hospital said, my eyesight isn't bad for a gent of my years.

The National Health Service . . . We are too many. And yes, some patients have to wait a long time for treatment. In the old days they didn't wait, they just died.

Incidentally, what happened to fruit, fresh fruit? Remember it? What befell, quite recently, the Cox's orange pippin? Now all apples are of the same colour, shape and size, and have the same flavour, i.e. none. Getting juice out of a pear is hardly more difficult than getting blood out of a stone. Oranges with inviting outsides have little inside but pith. I remember when I was a kid how . . .

Ah, the glorious past! 'Then there's the age of Anne. What a wonderful time, Pope and Addison! So civilized, so cultivated. Their routs and their tea-parties and rapes of the lock': Lucia in E. F. Benson's *Mapp and Lucia*, 1935. The good old days. In the late nineteenth century a respected, male novelist-to-be, a disciple of Flaubert, Turgenev and the Goncourts, earned a living for some years as the editor of *Woman*, 'scribbling fashion notes under the name of "Gwendolen" and romantic idylls under the name of "Sal Volatile"'. (For this and much else, see John Gross: *The Rise and Fall of the Man of Letters*.)

The inglorious present! It's difficult not to feel anger. But keep

Ulrich's thought in mind: that you can't be angry with your own time without damage to yourself.

If worn under a dressing-gown or overcoat, pyjamas might get by as reasonable garb for a cystoscopy, but my wife reminds me that I'm on my way to the eye clinic at Bolingbroke Hospital, not the urological day clinic at St George's. I've got the dates mixed. Ought to feel relieved, but don't. At the eye clinic my pyjamas are found out of place, and I am dressed in a pair of velvety blue trunks. Unfortunately there don't seem to be any eye specialists available. I wait, though there's nowhere to wait. The hospital is much darker than I remember it, like a stage castle fallen into ruin. I drift into a large room, solid, comfortable, well-lit, full of armchairs, where an ophthalmologist is giving a lecture to an audience of ophthalmologists, and am firmly ejected. A kindly nurse takes me for a spin in her car to pass the time, and confides a long sad story of how her first love came to naught and she has never loved since.

Back at the hospital, and a small, plump, dandyish man pops up, takes a cursory look at me, and mutters 'It is not well.' He must be a foreigner; so many are. He holds up a sheet of paper, and tells me to read off the letters. It appears to be a restaurant menu, with the names of the dishes written in convoluted and swirling script, and I can't make out a thing. It's not fair! I grab at the sheet . . .

But I am exhausted. So exhausted that I wake up, in the usual worried sweat. Having pulled myself together, I reach for the morning paper, and read about a coffin wrapped in brown paper and bearing the inscription, 'Return to Sender'. This makes me feel better.

'Diseases desperate grown, By desperate appliances are reliev'd.' The cystoscope (cyst: Gk *kustis* bladder) is a flexible tube which bends this way and that ('looping the loop,' one merry operator told me), peering into every nook and cranny of the bladder. At its further end are a camera, an intense white light, a device for snipping and retrieving small removals, and (for all I know – I avert my eyes as I hear the thin hose being unwound) other Lilliputian instruments. The operator sees all through an attached monocular, and may choose to distract the patient (who needs distracting: what would happen if he started to squirm or pull away?) by displaying the glorious multicoloured turbulence on a sort of television screen above his head. All this – and the shooting down of any suspect tumour – is blessedly achieved without surgical intervention from outside. The only snag is getting the cystoscope into the bladder, and that too is remarkable, and no doubt aptly chastening, if not quite as neatly as in the case of the Earl of Gloucester and his bastard son: 'The dark and vicious place where thee he got/ Cost him his eyes.'

The operation has its nasty moments; only moments. Yet George Santayana proposed, 'Nothing can so pierce the soul as the uttermost sigh of the body.' And Marvell's Soul confessed, 'I feel, that cannot feel, the pain.'

In a newspaper piece of 1977, Primo Levi observed ('what everybody observes') that our dreams can be heavy with significance for us but are plain nonsense for other people. The person who recites his dreams 'is no less a nuisance to his listeners than the person who boasts of his aristocratic lineage, or who simply makes a great noise when he blows his nose'.

Since coming on this harsh verdict, I have not recorded any dreams. More, I have had no dreams. Now I feel blocked up, I have become a nuisance to myself.

('And what sort of interpretation of dreams is it,' Joseph Brodsky has asked, 'if it's not filtered through good old Ziggy?' True, that's the way to make dreams more acceptable in polite society.)

On the first occasion I'd managed with difficulty to locate the books

– books I badly wanted to consult, I knew nothing about their contents, only that they were precious to me, much needed. But the bell rang, the lights dimmed, the library (sounds like the long-lost London Library) was closing. The second time, some weeks later, I knew – I remembered – which way to turn, and pushed my way through a crowd of young people drinking from cans of Coca-Cola and the like. Then I found a curtain had been drawn across the corridor; a harpsichord recital was in progress, someone motioned me away.

The dreams are flowing again. Perhaps in a third instalment I'll lay my hands on those books, the books that will mean so much to me.

Christopher Leach tells me of overhearing an old lady in the market: 'I have to get my painkillers on suspicion these days.' Can't say I blame her.

'*Please read this leaflet carefully. Keep it since you may want to read it again.*'
'You should not take the tablets if you are pregnant or planning to become pregnant, or breast-feeding, or have had reactions to similar medicines such as difficulty in breathing or swallowing, swelling of the hands, feet, face, lips, tongue or throat. You should consult your doctor if you have problems with your liver or kidneys, are on a low-salt diet, or are suffering from diabetes, loose bowels, vomiting, or low blood pressure (characterized by fainting and dizziness), or are receiving treatment for an allergy to bee or wasp stings. The tablets may affect your ability to drive a car or operate machinery, so you should not perform such tasks until you know whether or not you are able to do so.

'Like all medicines, your tablets can have unwanted effects, among them light-headedness, dry mouth, rashes (with or without itching), psoriasis, sensitivity to sunlight, joint and muscle pains, pins and needles, abdominal bloating, ringing in the ears, diarrhoea, constipation, sleepiness, inability to sleep, strange dreams, running nose, wheezing, the production of no or less urine, black stools, heartburn, jaundice, hair loss, weight gain, larger breasts, changes in the way things taste, impotence, confusion, decrease in mental agility.

'Do not be alarmed at this list. For more exhaustive answers to your questions concerning your condition, free booklets are available from the address given below.'

To sum up: If way to the better there be, it exacts a full look at the worst.

In connection with their antibiotic, Amoxil, SmithKline Beecham Pharmaceuticals warn us that we should see our doctor straight away 'if you notice your urine becoming darker or faeces (otherwise known as poo) becoming paler'. (Otherwise known as other things.) More poignantly, Asta Medica's painkiller, Zamadol, 'may cause feelings of sadness'.

'Language has lost the very capacity for truth, for political or personal honesty,' George Steiner declares. He adduces the designation 'Operation Sunshine' for a thermonuclear detonation. Yet even its inventors – cut-price PROs? – couldn't seriously have believed that it would conceal the truth for long or deceive anyone who wasn't ready to be deceived. The epithet, ostensibly grandiose, breezy and self-congratulatory, carries an ironic charge, less than subtle, which the inventors let by (perhaps as a face-saver) since they assume that the common man wouldn't recognize irony if it shone right in his face. In fact language has here prevailed, with ease, over its users and abusers.

But talk of the dishonesty and deceptiveness of words is metaphorical: we are talking about ourselves, we are the weasels. Words in themselves are neither honest nor dishonest. It is we who, in Eliot's phrase, slip and slide. We say that words 'fail us', when we don't have the time or the patience or the inclination to lay our hand or tongue on the right word, and our thinking goes astray. Except perhaps in mystical connections, the right word or combination is generally within reach. The failure, the fault, is ours. We live with it; we are imperfect creatures; if the absolutely right word doesn't exist it's because we haven't known the need for it.

(I rather regret embarking on this subject. I fear I have failed words.)

Yet if words can express everything, what is music, that lexiconless language, for?

In age, they say, one's reading becomes more selective. Untrue, in my experience. Except in this respect: one can't reach books stacked on the top shelves, one daren't lower oneself to those on the bottom shelves, heavy books are out of the question, as also those with small or faint print. So yes, one's reading becomes more selective.

'Ein alter Mann ist stets ein König Lear.' In one respect at least: Would you be kind enough to undo this button?

Books have their fates. Frank Kermode, knight, literary critic and former Professor of English, was moving house, and had boxes of books, inscribed first editions and valuable manuscripts, ready for the removal men. The three workmen to whom he showed the boxes were Cambridge dustmen called in to make a special waste clearance. Thirty boxes had been consigned to the dustcart before the mistake was realized. The dustmen declined to climb into the cart, which contained a mechanical crusher. A peculiarly cruel fate – let's have no cheap talk of irony – cruel to the books, to their owner, and to book lovers in general.

That hard-pressed organ, developed over a lifetime, which seeks out consolations calls to mind Patricia Beer and how, as her house was burning down, she ran inside to save a book or two and came out clutching the family cat.

It was generally understood (see *Who's Who*, *The Oxford Companion to English Literature*, contributors' notes in anthologies, and so forth) that Patricia Beer was born in 1924. The obituaries, however, give 1919, which seems less likely on the face of it or of her. If they can be wrong about the date of birth, they can be wrong about the date of death. As Patricia says in the introduction to her *Collected Poems*, 'a Collected Poems is a way of saying "I am not really dead."'

A leaflet announces a new magazine 'for women who write', called *Mslexia*. Explanations are necessary: '"Mslexia" means women's writing (ms = woman, lexia = words). But its association with dyslexia is intentional. Dyslexia is a difficulty, more prevalent in men, with reading and spelling. Mslexia is a difficulty, more prevalent in women, with getting into print.'

A clever invention, even though dyslexia is a real disability, caused by a condition of the brain. I first encountered it in Singapore, in the essays of a woman student whose grasp of the subject was sound but whose spelling was not. As if in extenuation, she confessed that she was married and had a child – but would I please keep this secret since she didn't want to be 'different' or treated differently from the other girls, who were all unmarried and nominal (I'd say actual) virgins. Just possibly she was hoping to be treated a wee bit differently when it came to the exams. I had a word with her tutor.

The launch issue of the new magazine will include, not unpredictably, a section of erotic writing (these women don't want to be read differently from men) and an article by a bestselling novelist contending that 'the selflessness of motherhood may be at odds with the self-absorption of the committed author'. Also promised are 'fool-proof exercises to get the creative juices flowing'. It should be noted that the leaflet is entirely free from msprints, msspellings, msrepresentations and overt msandry.

Women have the right to write, and many do. Whether we are men or women, when it comes to 'getting into print' a number of factors are involved, including the right of other people not to be dragged into print. Once we start to talk about human rights, there is no end to it. Often there ought to be, and promptly.

Last year Dennis Nilsen, serving life imprisonment for the murder of twelve men, claimed in the High Court that he was the victim of discrimination and abuse of his human rights. While heterosexual soft porn circulated freely among heterosexual prisoners, his favourite homosexual magazine was banned by prison staff. Such treatment, said his barrister, was 'inhuman and degrading': 'To deny the claimant expression of his sexuality because it is of a homosexual nature is cruel.' Has the High Court nothing better to do with its time? Prison, we take it, is meant to have its inconveniences, but discrimination between sexual tastes won't do, so the answer must be: ban all porn, whatever its complexion. One wonders what language Nilsen's defence would have found, had circumstances differed, to deplore the violation of the human rights of the men he had killed.

Sixteen days later, the press reported on a case equally absurd but far more cruel, apropos of which we would be almost justified in maintaining that words fail us. For the past year a ninety-three-year-old widow, living in sheltered accommodation, had been helped every morning by a female carer to wash herself. Then officials of South Gloucestershire Council phoned her to say that her usual carer was being replaced by a man. When she protested that she found this embarrassing, she was warned that she might be asked to see a psychiatrist to discuss her 'problem with men', and she could lose her home help altogether. A relative who interceded was told that it would be an infringement of the male worker's human rights not to allow him to carry out the bathroom duties. Finally a spokesperson for the Council, failing to conceal her irritation, stated that social services officials were that very moment trying to resolve the dispute. One should fight one's corner, but it's worrying that those most energetic in pursuing their rights are quite often – and, one might think, plainly – in the wrong. But then, to see what is in front of one's nose, George Orwell said, requires a constant struggle.

Children and animals, the remaining simpletons, the tongue-tied, have the right to rights. (But what is happening to some of our children?) For the rest of us, there are wishes and hopes.

Some while back, when I could still manage the walk in two stages, I paused to rest a while at the bus shelter, my halfway house. A young woman was pressing a mobile phone (they were not yet ubiquitous) to her ear, listening intently. When she turned as if watching for a bus, I noticed that the phone was an arrangement of clothes pegs clipped together. Presentably dressed in the drab garments favoured by her generation, reasonably good-looking, sober of mien, she exhibited none of the commoner signs of mental disorder. Perhaps she was simply keeping up with the Joneses – and well beyond the old fellow sharing the shelter, apparently immobile and going nowhere, with only an old walking-stick to boast of. Suddenly the young woman slipped the phone into a capacious pocket and bounded purposefully away. The clothes pegs must have conveyed some urgent message.

Having reached the Chinese restaurant, I sat down comfortably to wait for a takeaway. I picked up a magazine called *Elle*; on the cover it promised '21st CENTURY SEX. Your life and loves in the next millennium'. I dropped it hastily and picked up another, Asda's free magazine: 'Bright Young Things', and 'Win a Free Trip to Florida'. I tried again. Ah, a Chinese magazine. At least I could understand some of the cartoons.

*

'Praise my soul, the King of heaven . . .' This was how in those far-off days I parsed that famous opening line, wondering what cause he had to do so. I vaguely supposed (looking back, I have the impression that most things were vague suppositions) that I had something called a soul, but it didn't strike me as notably praiseworthy. All the others in church were making the same demand or request, and with full-blooded confidence. (There were lots of people then, when I was earning 3d a month as an unskilled or makeweight choirboy on Sunday mornings.) Had I considered the matter more deeply, it might have occurred to me that since (it appeared) God had created our souls he was really praising himself. As it was, I joined in, conscientiously earning my pay. Later I was getting 6d, and had ceased to speculate on the exact meaning of what I was singing. Knowing the tune was enough. Then one of us died, the most angelic-looking, the best-behaved, and we were called on to perform at his funeral service. 'Safely, safely gathered in, far from sorrow, far from sin.' A small coffin, weeping parents: reality had burst into the church. Was it for me, having got the hang of the punctuation, to praise this King? – who, the story went, had saved from weary strife, in its dawn, this fresh young life. Soon afterwards my voice broke, as did some other things.

God gave his only begotten son . . . Yes, but why such a fuss about it? God could beget other sons, as many as required. In a poem entitled 'Easter' Sisson puts his lugubrious finger on the truly momentous thing: 'What is astonishing is that he came here at all/ Where no one ever came voluntarily before.' That's more like it.

On the subject of what we call emotional blackmail: Gide tells of a small boy whose pious Protestant parents were forever drumming into him the meaning of the Crucifixion. Just think, they hung Jesus on a cross and hammered nails through his hands – all done for you – hammered nails through his poor hands! At last the boy rebelled: 'They had to, else he wouldn't have stayed up there.'

Samuel Butler opined that if Christ could be said to have died for him, it was in the same sort of way as the London and North Western Railway had been made for him. He was very glad that the railway was made, but did not suppose the builders had him in mind at the time. 'The debt of my gratitude is divided among so many that the amount due from each one is practically nil.'

'No mention of God for long enough. They keep him up their sleeve for as long as they can, vicars, they know it puts people off': 'A Lady of Letters', Alan Bennett's *Talking Heads*. My copy of *Brewer's Dictionary of Phrase and Fable* (1981) informs us that the word 'God' probably comes from an Aryan root *gheu*, to invoke, adding that 'it is in no way connected with *good*'. Nice to have an authoritative ruling.

That God doesn't exist, or died some while back, is no excuse. 'God is the only being who, to reign, wouldn't even need to exist': Baudelaire. Recently a disabled British schoolboy in Lourdes on pilgrimage was hit by a bus and died. After enumerating various unfairnesses visited on the faithful – 'Many of those who now lie rotting away/ Had faith in you' – Brecht's 'Hymn to God' concludes

Many of us say you are not – and a good thing too.
But how could *that* thing not be which can play such a trick?
If so much lives by you and could not die without you –
Tell me how far does it matter that you don't exist?

When told by the chaplain that they were in God's hands, Mother Courage hoped things were not as desperate as that.

It's difficult to escape religion altogether. Admitted to hospital, a woman was answering the mandatory questionnaire. Asked about her religion, she replied, 'None'. After a moment's hesitation the nurse wrote down 'Nun'. Strangely affecting is a story attributed to Groucho Marx, about a man saying grace in a low voice, and someone at the table interrupting him: 'I can't hear you.' The man said, 'I'm not talking to you.'

A rather splendid knock-down argument comes from Pascal: 'We must be born guilty or God would be unjust.' God is his own interpreter, and he will make it plain.

Letters to the Editor. A Corkonian notes that a weather forecast for the Republic of Ireland speaks of 'freshening southerly winds with ales in exposed parts later'. ('Hardy lot those Irish, drinking outdoors in such wet and windy weather.') Someone else reports that his photocard driving licence, recently issued by the Driver and Vehicle Licensing Agency, gives his place of birth as 'Untied Kingdom'. Goethe's remark comes to mind again: When he saw a misprint he always thought something new had been invented.

So many writers, so many great writers, and lots of them with foreign names! A *TLS* proof hints at how to shorten the roll-call: 'Nietzolstoy'. God preserve us, it's almost always a mistake to take the name of God, in vain or otherwise. Even as one of those 'vacant metaphors' that 'rattle about like old rags or ghosts in the attic', as George Steiner has it. General Wesley Clark surmised that for President Milošević, facing the vast air power deployed against him 'must be like fighting God' (press report, 12 May 1999). Since General Clark was Supreme Allied Commander at the time, this might seem a somewhat presumptuous declaration. Not, God forbid, that the General likened himself to the Almighty exactly, or only by implication. For God had appointed his son as supreme commander during that hectic if short-lived strife in heaven: 'the glory may be thine/ Of ending this great war, since none but thou/ Can end it.'

Rattling about like old rags . . . The modern rag trade calls on the ancient vocabulary of religion: 'Long the Holy Grail of fashion, the perfect pair of jeans is finally attainable.' See also a reference in *The Times* to the Perrier Award as 'stand-up comedy's Holy Grail', the same organ's greeting of the newly appointed rugby coach for the British Lions with the headline 'Guide us O thou Great Redeemer', and a BBC journalist's description of the Heineken Cup as Rugby Union's 'Holy Grail'. The Grail is mass-produced these days.

Can it be that, like Milton (the justifier of his ways), God spoke a form of what, in the fullness of time and after a number of backslidings, became the more or less universal language of our earthly world?

According to Dante, the first human to speak in words was Eve, when conversing with the serpent. He found it worrying that 'an act so noble for the human race' came from the lips of a woman rather than those of a man. But, as Umberto Eco points out, presumably Adam made some sort of sounds when naming the animals, and also when showing his satisfaction at the sight of Eve. (Sounds more refined, we trust, than animal grunts.) Possibly Dante meant that the conversation Eve had with the serpent was the first *dialogue* recorded in Genesis. The sad implication here is that Adam was not only naked and unashamed but also tongue-tied at home. Or couldn't get a word in.

If anything, Eco says, we know that it was God who first spoke in Genesis while creating the world: 'And God said, Let there be light' and so forth. And God spoke to Adam, forbidding him to eat of the tree of knowledge of good and evil. What form did his utterance take? Tradition has imagined 'a sort of language of interior illumination' wherein God expressed himself by thunderclaps and lightning (cf. Cowper: He 'rides upon the storm'); that is, he spoke in a loud voice and his eyes flashed.

Wouldn't the first language, this gift from God to Adam, have been Hebrew? (A reader of *The Times* informs us that his great-grandmother devoted her declining years to learning Hebrew on the grounds that it was the most likely language to be spoken in heaven, and she would need it to get around.) But no, that first language was lost after the Babel débâcle. Eco mentions 'the naïve belief that one's own tongue is the only existing and perfect one'. 'Naïve' derives from *nativus*, native; it is native to us to believe our native language the perfect – or least imperfect – one. 'The words were all before them, which to choose./ Their tongues now turned to English,/ With its colonies of twangs./ And they were down to earth': thus a naïve chauvinist's view of post-Edenic discourse.

Naïve isn't the word for Georg Philipp Harsdörffer, who claimed in 1641 that the German language 'speaks in the language of nature ... thunders with the heavens, flashes lightning with the quick moving clouds, radiates with the hail, whispers with the wind' and so on. Moreover German roars like the lion, snarls like the bear, bleats like the sheep, grunts like the pig, honks like the goose, chirps like the sparrow, barks like the dog, miaows like the cat, hisses like the snake ... All of which would have helped Adam immensely in naming the animals, since he could express 'in a manner conforming to their nature, each and every innate property and inherent sound'. Totally and immediately germane, in fact.

The Egyptians used to believe they were the most ancient of all the races in the world. According to the Greek historian Herodotus, one of their kings sought to determine the question by experiment. He took two newly born infants from their parents and gave them to a shepherd to be brought up among his flocks, commanding that no one should speak a word in their presence. They lived in a secluded cottage, and the shepherd fed them and looked after their needs in silence. One day, some two years into the experiment, as the shepherd entered the cottage, both children ran up to him, their hands outstretched, and uttered the word 'becos'. Inquiries showed that this was the Phrygian for 'bread'. The Egyptians were forced to concede that the Phrygians were more ancient than they.

In Nice, in 1943, the playwright Tristan Bernard (author, incidentally, of *L'Anglais tel qu'on le parle*) met the child Gabriel Josipovici, and learnt that the first word he had uttered was 'ish': 'man'. Bernard smote his forehead and exclaimed (in French), 'I knew it! Living proof that Hebrew is the original language!' (See 'Nice, 1943', *London Magazine*, August/September 1999.)

' . . . their love letters chart their agonies and ecstasies so intimately, it feels like eavesdropping to read them': promotional material for a public reading in the King's Head Theatre, Islington. The theatre boasts an induction coil, perhaps the sort of device used in surveillance, which makes eavesdropping easier for those hard of hearing.

Vernon Scannell and I swap misconceptions, visual and auditory. He noticed a reference in the *Radio Times* to 'the Bonker Prize-winning writer'. In Southfields Library, my eyes fell on a book with the title *Cold is the Gravy*, a piece of stark social realism, I supposed, somewhat outmoded: a closer look revealed it to be a thriller, *Cold is the Grave*; a newspaper referred to 'Tony Blair's sex change' (no, just that boring old sea change). Vernon mentions his surprise and excitement on hearing a Radio 3 announcement that Haydn's Piano Sonata in E Minor was about to be played by Captain Scott; turning to the *Radio Times*, he was sadly let down to find that the pianist was Kathryn Stott. My mishearings tend to the crudely sensational: 'a tax on parsnips' (payslips); 'we can expect a number of murders in the media world' (merely mergers, alas); 'returning from holiday, Ken Livingstone, the Mayor of London, was battered to death' (back at his desk).

Creative misunderstanding. 'The very deaf, as I am, hear the most astonishing things all around them, which have not, in fact, been said. This enlivens my replies until, through mishearing, a new level of communication is reached': Henry Green, in the course of an interview for *The Paris Review*, 1958.

In his early years Peter Vansittart was an avid reader, not unduly bothered as to whether or not he truly understood what he was reading. The author of *The Scarlet Pimpernel*, could 'Baroness' be her Christian name? The expression 'Master of the Horse' intrigued him – was there only one horse? – and a chapter heading, 'Louis Napoleon flees from Ham', came alive when he thought of school meals. It may have struck him – and he so young – that getting things right could be more hazardous than getting them wrong: when a question was asked in class and he came up with the correct answer, 'Jesus', the master misheard it as 'Jeeves', and he was beaten for irreverence.

During that same interview Henry Green was asked what he thought of the idea that his work was 'too subtle' for American readers.

INTERVIEWER: How about subtle?

MR GREEN: I don't follow. *Suttee*, as I understand it, is the suicide – now forbidden – of a Hindu wife on her husband's flaming bier. I don't want my wife to do that when my time comes – and with great respect, as I know her, she won't . . .

INTERVIEWER: I'm sorry, you misheard me; I said, 'subtle' – that the message was too subtle.

MR GREEN: Oh, *subtle*. How dull!

Vernon Scannell passes on two howlers remembered from his days as a prep-school teacher. In a test on figures of speech, a definition of 'simile': 'like a laugh but you don't make any noise'; and in a general knowledge test, a rather common and innocent confusion: 'an octopus is a sea creature with eight testicles'. An academic of my acquaintance (no names, no pack-drill) reports a rare locution in an essay criticizing William Blake: 'hippocracy'. Possibly a pious student's scandalized reaction to the hellish proverb, 'The tygers of wrath are wiser than the horses of instruction.' In *The Times* Philip Howard picks out the best of the season's howlers: 'the streets of Pompeii were full of red hot saliva', and 'born of the Virgin Mary, deceived of the Holy Ghost'. Not so subtle was the mobilization officer interviewing a promising recruit in 1942. Asked what languages he knew, the recruit said that besides speaking several languages he could read hieroglyphics. 'What are hieroglyphics?' asked the officer. 'The language of the Pharaohs, sir.' The recruit was accordingly posted to a Field Security Section in the Faeroe Islands. This brings to mind the GCSE bloomer (frequently cited: does this make it more likely to be authentic or less?): 'Ancient Egypt was inhabited by mummies and they all wrote in hydraulics.'

Other GCSE specimens demonstrate this desperate grasping after words heard only once before, or misheard. 'Solomon had three hundred wives and seven hundred porcupines'; 'Voltaire invented electricity' (a brilliant inference, worth half marks); 'Shakespeare's plays are all written in Islamic pentameters'; 'Bach practised on an old spinster which he kept up in the attic'; 'Moses went up on Mount Cyanide to get the ten commandments. He died before he ever reached Canada.' Interesting to see which words young people are unfamiliar with, and even more interesting to see which they are familiar with.

'Cervantes wrote Donkey Hote': much can be forgiven when foreign words are in question. Even a yuppie computer's insistence on rendering 'Keeper of the Quaich' (an honour in the world of whisky, 'quaich' being a Scottish drinking-cup) as 'Keeper of the Quiche'. Less forgivable in the circumstances was the person responsible for a newspaper advertisement for Brittany Ferries: 'Bistros and brassieres line up and welcome you to a continental way of life.' It's hardly an improvement if you happen to know that in France a 'brasserie' (stirring the brew with 'les bras', the arms) is a pub, a 'brassière' is a baby's vest with long sleeves, while what we call a bra is, in their more majestic expression, a 'soutien-gorge'.

More willing than most organs to admit to its follies, the *Guardian* was prompt to correct a homophonic-type error in an item about unexploded bombs: ' . . . as soon as our engineers figured out how to diffuse one lot, a more sophisticated version dropped from the skies'.

Excusable if mortifying was the misplaced zeal of the woman police constable who, alerted by radio to a fax and phone gone missing, arrested a passer-by carrying a saxophone. Was it a hazy, unhappy thought of 'pie in the sky' that inspired George W. Bush's avowal that 'The future will be better tomorrow'? Excitement (or conceivably wit) may have sparked off an Olympic Games commentator of some years back: 'That bronze medal is worth its weight in gold!' And mischief could be responsible for a notice displayed at Spey Bay Golf Club: 'Any persons (except players) caught collecting golf balls on this course will be prosecuted and have their balls removed.' I see that my last book (no, my most recent), *Signs and Wonders*, crops up in a note in a reissue of the *Oxford Book of Death* as *Science and Wonders*. May do sales some good.

But then, we don't bother much with words. They mean what we want them to, or we license them to mean equivocally (as in a newspaper headline: 'Shell's £4 bn investment plans will increase lead in new fuels'), or they mean next to nothing, they just have a snazzy ring to them. A driving school does business under the name 'Impact School of Motoring' as well as running a coach-hire service; a travel company specializing in 'Summer Sun' and 'Winter Sun' holidays is pleased to call itself 'Eclipse'.

Only today my eyes fell on the words 'Robin Day', and for a moment I thought how nice, this much loved bird had been commemorated, along the lines perhaps of the American Groundhog Day. (The context must have dissolved into a mist.) Who knows what murky half-thoughts or blurred atavistic memories were infiltrating somebody's mind when *The Church of England Newspaper* reported that the Archbishop of York, visiting a new refectory at Walsingham, 'unveiled a plague on the building', or a mail order catalogue offered 'Calvary twill trousers'. When Vernon Scannell gave a reading at a posh girls' school in Malvern, one of his poems made reference to Golgotha. None of them had heard of it, so he suggested that they might recognize it in its Latin form, Calvary.

The young ladies gazed back at him with refined perplexity. 'Then one of them lifted a tentative finger. I said, "Ah, good! You know Calvary." She said, "It means soldiers on horseback." ' It is less easy to smile over the response of a friend's ten-year-old son to a question asking what we call 'the period between the ages of about 11 and 15 when the body rapidly changes and develops'. The answer came: purgatory.

In *The Times*, mark you, Matthew Parris tells us that he finds the television programme *Big Brother* 'by turns teasing, titivating and gripping'. Ah well, tits in both. More interestingly, the *Independent* recently announced that in villages west of Amiens 'horses have been winnowing in a panicky way'. *The Times* again: apropos of 'Nasty' Nick Bateman, lately a contestant in *Big Brother*, we read that 'pampering to the former stockbroker's fifteen minutes of fame', publishers are offering big advances for a 'lightning' biography of him. Was Pamparus another seedy uncle of Cressida's, perhaps? From the same 'paper of record' we gather that David Trimble won 'the Noble Peace Prize'.

Highly comical, no doubt. Less so was an examination board's error in simple arithmetic. Pupils sitting a business studies paper were asked to answer 'all nine questions': there were eleven of them. Who is to examine the examiners?

In a front page story about Mo Mowlam's intention to quit Parliament, a Downing Street spokesman denies that the Prime Minister had been irritated by her popularity with the party and the public or other lapses from etiquette. 'Such allegations are wholly salacious and 24-carat rubbish.' Salaciousness is not something one would readily associate with Dr Mowlam or indeed with Mr Blair. Possibly an error in transmission, and 'fallacious' was meant. As also an advert in the *West Briton*: 'Competent chef required by quality restaurant . . . No time wasters or pre-Madonnas.'

Mr Jeremiah Cruncher, the odd-job man in *A Tale of Two Cities*, 'always spoke of the year of our Lord as Anna Domino apparently under the impression that the Christian era dated from the invention of a popular game, by a lady who had bestowed her name upon it'.

It was with some reluctance that I referred to the lady as Mo Mowlam, but that is how she is commonly known and presumably content to be.

There are times when it seems one must be living in a parallel universe. The reviewer (female, young) of a reprint of Q. D. Leavis's *Fiction and the Reading Public*, first published in 1932, tells us that such was the author's struggle in a male-dominated establishment to get the book published that she was discouraged from ever trying to write another. The enemies of promise in this case could be said to be the Cambridge English Faculty (male-dominated, but equally or more hostile to her husband, and both of them gave at least as good as they took), ill health, and (though she would never have advanced this, let alone lamented it) bringing up three children.

In fact publishers, albeit predominantly male at the time, were eager for further books from Mrs Leavis. Besides essays printed mainly in *Scrutiny* on Jane Austen, Henry James, Edith Wharton, George Eliot, Margaret Oliphant, Charlotte and (at length) Emily Brontë, and others, she contributed over 250 pages to the book, *Dickens the Novelist*, written in collaboration with F. R. Leavis.

The reviewer, recoiling from the male-dominating married name, refers to the author as 'Queenie'. If ever there was a woman you wouldn't even think of by her forename (even if it weren't what it happened to be) it was Q. D. Leavis.

Still, it's good that her name isn't totally forgotten, and that *Fiction and the Reading Public* has been reissued.

When the news broke of the closing down of the Oxford University Press's poetry list, I happened to be reading the second volume of

Richard Holmes's biography of Coleridge, specifically the story of the tinker's boy calling at the house in Highgate where Coleridge was staying, and asking if they had 'any old poets' in need of attention.

No point in rehearsing the rights and wrongs of the affair. On the side of the Press's bosses there were no rights at all, only ignorance, stupidity, hypocrisy, an open, possibly unprecedented contempt for a considerable body of their authors, and a general ineptitude beggaring description. The poetry editor, Jacqueline Simms, alone believed what she was saying. '*Cet animal est très méchant, Quand on l'attaque il se défend*': what gross impertinence! The Oxford bosses were aghast – a slip of a girl, a mere part-timer, answering back! She won a clear moral victory. The list was broken up and she lost her job.

The Concise Oxford Dictionary defines 'publisher' thus: 'a person or thing that publishes'.

'How vain painting is.' Pascal observed that painting excites admiration by resembling things whose originals we do not admire. Goethe viewed it from a slightly different angle: painting is the most indulgent of the arts, we let the poorest reproduction pass because we are used to seeing even sorrier original objects. Some such thought may have inspired Roland Barthes to claim: '*Écrite, la merde ne sent pas.*' If anything, it smells worse. If it honestly didn't smell when written, it wouldn't get written.

'The Chinese have never regarded novel-writing as anything more than a rather doubtful diversion for a literary man,' said Colonel Clement Egerton, the 1939 translator of the novel *Chin P'ing Mei* (*The Golden Lotus*) into English, or where deemed appropriate into Latin. Poetry has been another thing altogether. Discussing English versions of Chinese poetry, in 1983, David Hawkes judged that 'the erotic element is perhaps a little overplayed at times in these translations, partly because of Dr Birrell's choice of "loins" for *chang*, "bowels", which is where the Chinese thought their emotions were seated. I don't think strong feelings in the bowels were associated in any way with sex.'

Poetry readings are strange affairs. In the distant unregenerate past I would sense every now and then an instant air of indignant affront emanating from some close-knit poetry group, as if by a freak mishap their usually reliable secretary had invited quite the wrong speaker. Perhaps the most satisfying readings are those where (so you have been tipped off) Special Branch officers or their equivalents are to be present. For one thing, this makes the whole affair seem (rightly or wrongly) more meaningful; for another, you can be sure they won't draw attention to themselves by asking awkward questions. They'll be too busy trying to work out what you are driving at – just as you wish all listeners and readers would do. (A word of caution: you should choose your country with care.)

In his autobiography the German critic Marcel Reich-Ranicki quotes Martin Walser, novelist and satirical playwright, born 1927, as identifying the prototypical author with an Egyptian shepherd named Psaphon who taught the birds to sing his praises: a picturesque but lowering version of the view, ascribed to Coleridge, that every great and original writer must himself create the taste by which he is to be relished.

'Criticism is a goddess easy of access and forward of advance,' Johnson asserted in *The Idler*, 'who will meet the slow and encourage the timorous' – that's to say, a deity promiscuous in acquiring votaries and prodigal with her favours.

However, it is unwise to wax categorical on details of diction. In *The Rambler* Johnson took issue with Macbeth's (i.e. Lady Macbeth's) vehement invocation, 'a wish natural to a murderer':

> Come, thick night
> And pall thee in the dunnest smoke of hell,
> That my keen knife see not the wound it makes,
> Nor heav'n peep through the blanket of the dark,
> To cry, 'Hold, hold!'

– a passage in which, he says, all the force of poetry is exerted, yet its efficacy is destroyed by the intrusion of a low epithet, 'dun', seldom heard outside the stable. Today, stables having moved up-market, the word's ignominious association has evaporated; in fact the *Concise Oxford Dictionary*'s second definition describes it as '*poet.* dark, dusky' – with, quite likely, Shakespeare's use of the word in the forefront of the lexicographer's mind. The 'utmost extravagance of determined wickedness' that follows, Johnson continues, is debased by 'two unfortunate words' which tempt him to laughter: the avengers of guilt are represented as peeping through a blanket. (God or his agents as peeping Tom.) True, we are pulled up short, but only for a moment, such is the impetus of the lines. The other unfortunate word is 'knife', this being 'an instrument used by butchers and cooks in the meanest employments', so that we do not – or not at once – conceive that 'any crime of importance is to be committed with a *knife*', an object habitually involved in 'sordid offices'. Johnson might have preferred 'dagger' ('Is this a dagger which I see before me?' Macbeth asks a little later), but these days a knife is quite sufficiently dreadful: it is what throats are cut with, while daggers are largely confined to costume dramas.

It was Johnson's acute and fearful responsiveness to the sentiments of the passage and the energy of their expression that impelled him to incidental censures (perhaps an instinctive gesture of self-defence) which we incline to think comically misplaced. There is nothing here for us to exult over. Johnson notes, shrewdly and amusingly, that such 'imperfections of diction' will be wholly imperceptible to a foreigner whose knowledge of the language comes from books rather than active life, and less obvious to a 'solitary academic', unlikely ever to venture into a butcher's shop or a domestic kitchen, than to a 'modish lady' who keeps an extensive set of cutlery. (For example, Lady Macbeth herself, a notable hostess.)

'Karoline, you must read *Wilhelm Meister.*'

'Of course I have read *Wilhelm Meister,*' she said. Fritz was disconcerted for a few seconds, so that she had time to add, 'I found Mignon very irritating.'

'She is only a child,' cried Fritz, 'a spirit, or a spirit-seer, more than a child. She dies because the world is not holy enough to contain her.'

'She dies because Goethe couldn't think what to do with her next. If he had made her marry Wilhelm Meister, that would have served both of them right.'

A rousing piece of practical criticism, in Penelope Fitzgerald's *The Blue Flower*, feminine in forthright spirit rather than masculine, perhaps more British than German. Like the author, in fact.

Reviews of new novels are almost always laudatory. It would appear that the production of novels, whatever their subject-matter, is an outstandingly virtuous activity, of inestimable benefit to society. Seemingly novelists are blessed with human rights of a kind denied to writers in other genres. *The Times* (*Play*): ' . . . his propensity to employ pithy quotations from Shakespeare, Milton and Polonius one moment, and to revel in the comic joys of anal sex a hair's breadth later. It is bathos such as this, and much else besides in this accomplished book, that makes it such an unalloyed pleasure to read.' Neither literary nor literate. (Polonius, we suppose, is one of those famously deep Romans.) Increasingly reviewers sound like inferior blurb-writers.

*

The story is told of Angus Wilson, at work in his garden, hearing a passing child say, 'Look, Mummy, there's an old man writing.' The mother replied, 'Yes, darling, it does them so much good.' Indeed it does – even writing literary criticism, I dare say.

Have just turned down a kind request by the editor of the *Times Literary Supplement* to review a book published by Oxford University Press. Can't bring myself to touch any of their products, aside from ageing, prelapsarian dictionaries. An enticing subject, too: literary representations of the afterlife over the centuries. It might have done me so much good.

There are two simple reasons why people don't make good writers: (a) they have nothing to write about, (b) they are not at home with the written word (however fluent they may be in the spoken word). The latter is by far the more potent reason. If you can write, you'll find something to write about; having something to write about doesn't make you a writer.

Not that there is the slightest obligation to write, moral or social, as far as I can see. I have the deepest admiration and respect for people who can live perfectly well without writing, who get along without this crutch. (A crutch posing as a mission.) Unfortunately, writing – whether attended by the ability to write or not – seems to have joined those proliferating 'rights' which no one dare doubt, ignore, gainsay or waive.

Herodotus reported that the Massagetae, a nomadic people living to the east of the Caspian Sea, discovered a tree 'whose fruit has a very odd property'. When they held parties, they sat around a fire into which they threw some of it. It burned like incense, and the smell intoxicated them, so that they jumped up and danced and sang.

The Scythians used to creep into a little tent and throw hemp seeds on to a dish containing red-hot coals. They enjoyed the resulting vapour so much that they 'howled with pleasure'. This, Herodotus commented, was their substitute for bathing in water, which they never used.

In the late 1940s a group of students and staff from Farouk I University (later and more elegantly designated the University of Alexandria) toured the antiquities of Upper Egypt. Near Luxor a small cache of hashish was found in a boat plying the Nile. A hookah was sent for, and some damp coarse tobacco, and a local boy volunteered to prepare red-hot charcoal. A wild party ensued with loud laughter and cries of wonder. (No alcohol involved, of course, and with their customary discretion the young ladies made themselves scarce; so did the senior Egyptian staff.) The mouthpiece of the pipe passed from mouth to mouth: 'Very good exercise for the lungs!' A mini-lecture on the derivation of the word 'assassin' met with approbation.

The following morning a second cache was discovered. It seemed too good to be true, and a little research made it sadly plain that the small cakes of hypothetical hashish were dried pellets of Nile mud dropped from between the boatman's toes. Sobriety descended on us, and we returned our attention to the monuments of unageing intellect.

If a drug isn't addictive it can't be up to much. The question is, can the addiction be lived with? Opium smokers in Thailand in the 1950s – the only ones I've known – if they ate well, had a job and a family life, they got by. Prosperous businessmen (generally of Chinese stock) were said to become more prosperous, their wits sharpened by a few pipes; certain university teachers recruited from abroad marked exam scripts at twice normal speed and with rare equanimity (though a cautionary tale had it that on one occasion the scripts were left behind at the 'den' and used as spills). Opium was legal then, cheaper than beer, for all that the state took its modest impost. But the poor who couldn't afford food as well as opium, grew feebler, and hence more deeply addicted, and might in desperation attack passers-by for the coins in their pockets. (Such muggings never approached Western levels: the poor souls didn't have the strength.)

Remote from the squalid and febrile drug scene of our time and place. But the West never knew how to handle drugs. We were greedy, we expected too much (the Doors of Perception), and we gobbled them down like jelly babies. The wind must be tempered to the most shorn of lambs. The law protects the weakest, or seeks to. And addiction is a hazardous, unpredictable condition. So, no opium or cannabis for you, old fellow, no matter what relief it might bring.

Anthony Hecht speaks of university English departments (in America, as it happens) and 'the ill effects of interdisciplinary promiscuity'. A proposed course for schools was called 'Ebonics' (i.e. black street vocabulary). In the eastern parts of the US, Hecht remarks, educated Haitians, well-spoken and bilingual, are highly respected in the black community, which has led some less well-educated though well-intentioned mothers to name their sons 'Antwan'. (Not everyone is besotted with street vocabulary.) The given name of one black youth – 'Rayful' – puzzled Hecht and his wife until she worked out that it was meant to mean Raphael.

Hecht mentions a student of his who reckoned that 'limitations of technology' obliged Shakespeare to present the themes and emotions of his plays 'through the words of his characters'. Before long we shall have changed all that.

Anthony Hecht's poem 'Green: An Epistle' begins: 'I write at last of the one forbidden topic/ We, by a truce, have never touched upon . . .' In a lengthy interview with Philip Hoy – invoking this poem and Pascal's pensée, *'Le moi est haïssable'* – Hecht remarks that 'our capacity to think well of ourselves is versatile to the point of monstrosity'. Pride can disguise itself as humility; we can quietly pride ourselves on our quietness on this score, on what we choose to see as our modest and unassuming character. And then, 'the universal desire to think well of ourselves almost invariably involves the suppression of memory'.

Well, yes. But in age, it may be, 'le moi' is – until we forget everything – increasingly 'haïssable'. For one thing, the body, progressively unlikeable ('Le dernier acte est sanglant, quelque belle que soit la comédie en tout le reste': better leave this thought in its original language), is part and parcel of the 'moi'. For another, however faulty the mind grows, it tends to favour rather than suppress memories that in the hustle and bustle of earlier years were readily pushed aside: we forgot because we had to, now alas the compulsion has ceased. (Put it another way: 'When one trains one's conscience, it kisses while it bites,' said Nietzsche; but the time comes when the conscience forgets its training.)

Easy for Pascal to dismiss the self as hateful: he had something else to love. Hopkins implored, 'My own heart let me more have pity on; let/ Me live to my sad self hereafter kind,/ Charitable.' Harder done than said, but the sestet of the sonnet points to a possible, proper comfort: if for a night, a year, the poet lay wrestling, he was wrestling with God, not trading futile punches with his own sad self.

In the absence of God, the self – detestable but unmistakably there – is all we have. (Go carefully if it invades your writing, as it will.) Except, perhaps . . . But even to think of such precious, mortal fragilities seems foolhardy, let alone speak of them, or – a forbidden topic – write at last.

'If we wish to find ourselves, we must not descend into our own inwardness; it is only outside that we are to be found . . . None of us possesses his own self: it is wafted at us from without, escapes us for long periods and returns to us in a breath': Hugo von Hofmanns-thal. That's how it used to be. Inwardness, a suspect locale, was left to itself; it was by no means certain that we actually had anything as solid-sounding as a self. The books one read, the poetry – even (or especially) all of that lay 'outside'. (Richard Hoggart has written of the 'scholarship boys' of his and my generation: 'Like homing pigeons, to a loft we knew only from hearsay, we headed for the humanities and, above all, for literature.')

I hadn't left the house for a week or more. Now I walked to the chemist to photocopy a review, intending to drop in at the pub across the street, check the copy and post it forthwith. I joined an old lady waiting warily at the zebra crossing – our walking-sticks exchanged sympathetic nods – as a car sped in our direction. At the last moment the driver noticed the zebra crossing and us, and slammed on the brakes to let us cross. His car was struck by a car just behind. Recriminations followed, and the driver of the first car appealed for witnesses to testify on his behalf. The old lady was eager to oblige; for her the first driver was the hero – he had, if belatedly, stopped for us – and the second was the villain, travelling too fast and too close. In my view both drivers were speeding without due care and attention; the damage was minimal, only pride (which drivers tend to have in excess) had been hurt. Six of one and half a dozen of the other, I pronounced emolliently. A disgruntled silence fell, and I sloped off to the pub, firmly ordering a half-pint and spreading out my papers importantly.

My self, which had escaped me for quite some time, had returned to me in a breath, wafted on the smell of burnt rubber. No longer 'haïssable' (or plain boring), for a moment or two this 'moi' was positively pleasurable.

Macabéa, the poor, ignorant, innocent, ugly girl whom no one cares about, in Clarice Lispector's novel *The Hour of the Star*: 'I shall miss myself so much when I die.' Utterly unexpected, and so lucidly articulated for someone who could never find the right word.

Pascal talks about religion. Strange, then, that he should be so highly regarded by the laity and thought to be so astonishingly modern. But in many of his *Pensées* he does appear to be talking interestingly about quite other (and more 'relevant') things than religion. Why, some of his reflections might be addressed to critics and reviewers. 'One must have deeper motives and judge everything accordingly, but still talk like an ordinary person.' 'Two errors: (1) to take everything literally, (2) to take everything spiritually.' 'Nothing written simply for the author's benefit is any good.' 'When we read too quickly or too slowly we do not understand anything.' 'Continual eloquence is tedious.' 'If he exalts himself, I humble him. If he humbles himself, I exalt him.' 'Nothing shows more plainly the absurdity of a bad sonnet than to consider its nature and its model, and then to imagine a woman or a house conforming to that model.' 'No one is allowed to write well any more.'

Having read Pascal in some such spirit, one may be inspired to go back and reread him more attentively, as a writer on religious matters. A certain bathos is apt to ensue. 'I am one of those whom Pascal bowls over and doesn't convert,' said Albert Camus. To read him as seriously concerned with anything other than religion would have amazed Pascal (what could it be, this other to be seriously concerned with?) more than offended or distressed him. It should suffice that he had spoken sharply against those who misused Scripture by making the most of any passage which might dimly seem to support their erroneous views (or trivial concerns).

A nice title: 'Literary Remains in my Lifetime'. It's Musil's, no less, but for once I don't feel irresistibly disposed to steal it.

Epitaph: He trailed his coat, but nobody trod on it. (These days people are careful what they tread on.) Someone in the *TLS* ticks me off: '. . . is often facetious, which does not help in the difficult business of getting the English to like Goethe'. Was that what I was attempting? Serves me right, then.

A rise in the number of brutish-looking cars in the vicinity, with pet names like 'Fatboy', 'Raider', 'Shogun' and 'Trooper'. The new aesthetic: ugliness as an end in itself. A minor manifestation of 'Evil be thou my good.'

As also seen in TV commercials, increasingly ugly, coarse in a schoolboy fashion, postmodernly inconsequent or enigmatic. (Can it really pay off, leaving the viewer to work out what is being promoted?)

Schoolboy coarseness – I can't recall very much of it. Perhaps we were more easily embarrassed. The outstanding exception – though coarse isn't the word – was a boy at my elementary school, a combination of unwashed village idiot and serial rapist in the offing, given to gleeful flashing, not only in the playground where it might have passed ('there aren't any buttons on his pants'), but in the streets around. One day they ('They') took him away, and we didn't see him again.

A tribute to its inexorable power, we might suppose, that even those lost souls who knew nothing else, barely their own names, knew about sex and its mechanics – more than most of us reckoned *compos mentis* did at that age. Ignorance on this score was largely what *compos mentis* implied.

The curious sense, after crossing a not particularly busy road, even an empty road, that one has been hit by a car and killed, and the mind, a creature of habit, assumes in its last working moments that one has got safely to the opposite side and is going about one's intended business. The mark of a peculiarly glum nature, or of grotesque self-regard? I thought of this phenomenon, recurrent as it used to be, when reading a verse by Fergus Allen:

> No time is allowed for practice or rehearsal,
> There are no retakes and there isn't a prompter.
> There's only moving water, dimpled by turbulence –
> And no clambering out on to the bank
> To think things over, as there is no bank.

Any small discrepancies – moving water and turbulent dimples – are accounted for in the poem's title: 'To be Read Before Being Born'.

That look of grim determination, followed by bemusement, on the face of an old friend in the early stages of Alzheimer's: I'm going to get there if it kills me . . . but where is the there I'm going to get to?

To have gone through a lifetime believing that money wasn't everything – and then finding it is. A bit much.

Their bull gendereth, and faileth not, their cow calveth, and casteth not her calf . . . Like so many before him, Martin Amis claims that 'in the long term, literature will resist levelling and revert to hierarchy'. What matters is not what the ring of cattle dealers make out, but 'the decision of Judge Time', who constantly separates the sheep from the goats. (My mixed metaphor, not Martin Amis's.) We must do our best to forget what 'in the long term' can signify, or the voice of the less refined among us will be heard: 'I want it now.'

The magic word 'psychology'! (With its spellbinding associates, psychoanalysis, psychotic, psychopath, psychedelic, psychosexual . . .) A reviewer, himself famous in a similar line of fiction, commends Thomas Harris's *Hannibal* for its revelations concerning the psychology of the – er – hero, Dr (Cannibal) Lecter. He also refers to the 'high aesthetics' of the book's horrors – but who can be sure what the word 'aesthetics', high or low, is meant to mean here? With 'psychology', on the other hand, there's no cause for alarm.

A couple of days later Jack Straw, the Home Secretary, tells us we shouldn't be too downcast about the current decline in the popularity of marriage. We must remember that in the putative 'golden age' the death rate was much higher than nowadays, and marriages often didn't last long enough for the question of divorce to arise. (From that day forward till, quite soon, death did them part. An audacious act of spin-doctoring on Mr Straw's part.) So, as he says, no cause for alarm. The Government doesn't want us alarmed, doesn't want us to brood on the past. If we are encouraged to look back, it is only to make us look forward more keenly.

It is a mark of a caring society that the most outlandish practices are rendered safe. (Which can relieve pressure on the NHS.) Miss Cane, Miss Birch and the rest of the sorority, those therapeutic disciplinarians, are being urged to disinfect their whips after use. I doubt the thought crossed Nietzsche's mind as he drew up his advice: when you go among women don't forget to take your whip with you.

An actress whose husband has gone off with another actress, we hear, is suffering trauma. When was it – fairly recently – that the word 'trauma' suddenly soared into prominence, suavely invading our basic vocabulary? (In 1894 William James used the expression 'psychic *traumata*', between inverted commas, glossing it as 'thorns in the spirit, so to speak'. In 1984 the *Daily Telegraph* spoke of manufacturing industry as recovering only feebly 'from the traumatic experiences of the last five years'. Now, together with that ever-ready prefix, Post Traumatic Stress Disorder has been validated at the highest medical levels.

For some while, with the German 'Traum' in mind, I had idly supposed that 'trauma' had to do with dreams or nightmares. (Our word 'dream', by the way, is reported to come from Old English, 'joy, music'.) Straightforwardly enough, the dictionary defines 'trauma' as 'pathol. physical wound, physical shock following this; psychol. emotional shock following a stressful event, sometimes leading to long-term neurosis'.

In my childhood we knew nothing of pathology, neurosis or (apart from vague report) stress, and there was no psychology around. Our vocabulary, befitting circumstances and expectations, was limited. But – cometh the hour, cometh the word. Or contrariwise.

A delightful letter from Josefina, a Spanish Ph.D. student working on Lisa St Aubin de Terán: 'a hectic project of my mind'. She writes: 'Psychology seems to be a required element to clarify the hidden motives in the lives and relationships of those female characters embedded in a malestream of traditional culture.' (A rather splendid pun, 'malestream'/'maelstrom', though I wonder about 'embedded'.) Since, or so she has heard, I am 'one of the poets who best ally the magic of social commitment to the charm and inspiration of aesthetics' (cor!), she asks me to help her. I only wish I could. It would be nice to participate in the hectic project of someone's mind.

'This world cannot explain its own difficulties, without the assistance of another.' I can't recall the context of this resonant saying by the Revd Charles Caleb Cotton. Since it occurs in a compilation of 1820 entitled *Lacon*, it may well have no context, the Laconians (or Spartans) being famed for the terseness of their utterances. The suggestion appears to be that, if no other world is found to exist, we are inevitably beset by difficulties in explaining our difficulties – in any number of areas, if I may extrapolate, ranging across the good, the bad, the better, the worse, the best, the worst. Which in turn, considering our proficiency in explanation, suggests that there must be another world of sorts somewhere or other.

Have just undergone novation. Sounds like cosmetic surgery or a

75

new, demanding medical test. But no, my contracts for books of poems have been novated; a term quite possibly minted for this very occasion by a handy classicist with the word 'renovate' at the back of his mind: that is, with empty ceremony and self-satisfaction on the part of Oxford University Press, my books have been transferred from OUP to Carcanet Press. After sitting in one warehouse awaiting death, they will now be sitting in another and no doubt more hospitable one awaiting life.

In publishing during the 1970s, 'pipe-smoking fuddy-duddies' (the picturesque opprobrium of a whizz-woman waiting in the wings) at least did a spot of editing on authors' copy. Not, however on Iris Murdoch's novels. When I remarked on the absence of accents from scattered snippets of French, Norah Smallwood, our leader at Chatto & Windus and Iris's high priestess, would tell me not to intervene: this was sacred writ, all was meant. But perhaps the lady who typed the novels from Iris's longhand simply didn't have accents on her machine? Maybe, but 'Leave it as it is. If there are any mistakes we can blame them on the printers.' All the same, driven by some pig-headed, pipe-smoking vestigial sense of right and wrong, I quietly supplied missing accents and corrected any unmistakable mistakes. If I had transgressed, I could always blame it on the printers.

Jeremy Lewis indulges in hyperbole: so the severer type of critic might complain. The portraits in his memoir *Kindred Spirits* are surely exaggerated – heightened, let's say – as in the most effective caricatures, where embellishment or amplification (in Lewis's case, as good-natured as the facts allow, or more so) brings out plain truths.

'. . . far too sceptical, far too aware of the long-term, and far too committed to the highest standards, to have made a publisher, as opposed to a cautious and meticulous editor; left to his own devices he would have published, perhaps, two or three books a year, which might have made sense *sub specie aeternitatis* – if erring on the side of excess – but would never have paid the bills'.

Essentially true, alas. (More undeniably so than the nicer – do I mean even nicer? – things he says about me.) Then how come I ever entered publishing? Chiefly because I had happy memories of ten years of teaching in Singapore and of the friendly, virtually confederate relations between students and staff, and wasn't much taken with what I found in British institutions of higher learning. Immediately on returning in 1970 I did a couple of days a week tutoring first-year students in Leeds. It must have been on my first day there that one of them burst into my room, asking excitedly: 'Do you have any dirt on the VC?' I wasn't sure who the Vice-Chancellor was. (It was the widely admired Lord Boyle.) This wasn't my sort of war. Surely publishing would at least serve to keep sweet my memories of teaching literature, and see me through another ten years. Somehow 'Do you have any dirt on the MD?' didn't sound half so horrid.

Some reviewers observed that, besides being very funny, *Kindred Spirits* had historical value. It 'also says everything which needs saying about what has happened in publishing, and why' (Diana Athill, in *Stet*, which likewise says a good deal, in tones more plangent, on the same subject). Inadvertently its author was writing *sub specie aeternitatis*. (Thanks for the Latin ornament. Lewis's prose makes one's own look austere to the point of parsimony.)

'Everything was personalized and heightened: like a possessive, passionate parent, she bridled at any outside criticism of those within the fold and fought to defend her flock, but felt at liberty to cuff us about the head as briskly as she liked ... One of Norah's most effective techniques was to invoke the great names of the past, accompanied by a mournful shaking of the head and appropriate tut-tutting noises. Seeing herself as the guardian of a sacred flame,

"*Whatever* would Leonard [Woolf] think of that?" or "Cecil [Day Lewis] must be *turning in his grave*," she would intone.'

There is nothing over the top about Jeremy Lewis's portrayal of Norah Smallwood. In fact, for all its vividness, it is decidedly temperate. A technique he doesn't touch on was Norah's propensity to enlist Freud, one of our old authors, in the course of rebuke or disagreement. This was especially saddening in view of her intelligence and knowledgeability in other respects – reasons why staff who could afford to move out still stayed put. When I indiscreetly betrayed a fondness for my mother, she wagged a finger at me: 'Ha, ha, Oedipus!' And when I voiced my abhorrence of an American novel about a hyperactive necrophile given to killing courting couples and detaching the female and conveying her to his harem in a conveniently cool cave, she professed surprise that so kind and understanding a person as myself (i.e. a known softie) should fail to feel for a poor unfortunate who had no other way of communicating with people. She could only suppose (a twinkle in her eye) that deep down I harboured similar but suppressed desires. What those desires were I doubt Norah fully realized: just something a bit peculiar and rather vulgar. She was, in a Bloomsbury manner, broad-minded and also innocent.

(I rejected the book on the same day as a colleague visiting New York took it on for us. His opinion prevailed. The author, whose first novel it was, is now famous.)

Woman as Managing Director: 'She is wedded to convictions – in default of grosser ties;/ Her contentions are her children, Heaven help him who denies' (Kipling).

A curiosity touched on earlier . . . 'Lloyd finished the last chapter of his library book, and closed it with relief, wishing that it was in his power to abandon books halfway through.' However bad they were, 'he was obliged by some natural law to finish them'.

This confession comes in a book borrowed from my local lending library, *Redemption*, by Jill McGown. What accounts for the phenomenon? Slavish obedience to some childhood maxim? – Always finish what you've begun, Waste not, want not, If at first you don't succeed . . . A stubborn little feeling that the book should be given a second (third, fourth) chance? Nothing so rational can explain this perverse insistence on throwing good money (time is money) after bad. Something so unnatural must indeed be the outcome of a natural law. It casts light on that queer proverb, 'Beware beginnings'.

A proud boast. 'I don't need other people telling me what I should or shouldn't watch or read.' The Video Appeals Committee, consisting of intellectuals, has lifted the ban imposed by the British Board of Film Classification on seven pornographic videos, among them *Office Tart* and *Nympho Nurse Nanny*, thus allowing them to be sold in sex shops. The Committee appears to have adopted Tennyson's anguished cry as its slogan: 'Oh yet we trust that somehow good/ Will be the final goal of ill.'

Eyes holding up pretty well (or is it one nail driving out another?). Unfortunately I can read the headlines. 'Dying woman, 71, raped in hospital'.

'Tall and slim, gay male, 31, with brown hair, green eyes would like to meet a genuine fun guy, 18-35, to spend quiet nights in and crazy nights out with. Call me on Voice Box Number . . .' The two-page spread of dating ads in the local freesheet makes me think of an item in the Viennese newspaper, the *Neue Freie Presse*, 31 March 1900, as translated by Edward Timms in his book on Karl Kraus:

> *Travelling companion sought*
> young, congenial, Christian, independent.
> Replies to 'Invert 69' poste restante Habsburgergasse.

In those days you had to use your brains.

As one would expect, personal ads in the *London Review of Books* are culturally up-market – art galleries, theatres, bookshops and concerts of classical music feature prominently among the delights offered or looked for – and might well be written by would-be contributors with a measure of *savoir faire* and creative talent but insufficient earnestness or stamina to qualify for the other pages.

'Charming, pretty, intelligent, professional woman (forties) seeks unattached male for London cultural outings.' 'Gay Oxbridge bookaphile, 25, available to be taken away by rich uncle to Alfred Brendel's concert . . .' 'Clytemnestra seeks Agamemnon (40–45) with resolution to rewrite history.' 'Over-intellectual and bookish, passionate, pretty poet (male, 24) seeks over-intellectual, bookish, passionate older woman. Or anyone incredible.' '30 cigarettes a day and counting: 64-year-old male on the slow train to self-destruction and loving it would like to meet blonde, Danish woman, early twenties. That said, intelligent woman to 65 could still raise a laugh.' 'Happen to be gay? 34-year-old man in the book business, reasonably solvent, happy. Smokes, drinks and reads, all to excess. Now looking for an independent man with ready brain, ready laugh and tangential take on life.'

Reaction was bound to set in. 'I'm just a woman looking for love. Leave all this wordy wit . . .' 'Intimidated by George Eliot? With only half her intellect I'm still creative and wise, and much prettier.' 'Arty-farty, pretentious connoisseurs, intellectual wimps need not reply . . .' 'I used to be an idealist, now I'm just idle.' 'Bald art dealers are more sexy! London slaphead, 56, hates art (flogs imbecilic daubs to moneyed dolts), books (thinks Gutenberg invented a wine press), would like to meet semi-educated floozy half his age who delights in gin.' A resident of Bicester, a believer in experience rather than night classes, offers practical advice on the laws of survival: 'Don't smoke in bed, don't sleep in ashtrays.'

A paper in the north of England ran an advertisement on its 'Lonely Hearts' page which read: 'Professional man, 45, head on a stick, seeks similar woman.' When readers asked what freakish practice or rare condition was encoded in 'head on a stick', it emerged that a secretary in the office had taken the message over the phone, and what the man had intended was 'hedonistic'.

Publishers' statements grow increasingly long, detailed, and hard to decipher. However, it appears that during the past twelve months my books have earned not a penny. Balances are negative, largely owing to minus sales. (You mean you can sell fewer copies than none? Yes, when 'returns' trickle in. A friend sending a birthday card jokes uneasily about wishing me many happy returns.) They say that writing is like putting one's soul up for sale. That would explain things.

Ten per cent of what? I've been thinking of calling my agent and suggesting she drops me from her list of clients. We've been together for around fifty years. She's kind-hearted, and no doubt would reply with something bracing – about things picking up, let's not be hasty, wasn't I working on some sort of journal ... Being averse to melodramatics, I hadn't got round to it.

Until last night, that is. I stammered out my sad, noble piece, and silence ensued. Not a word of protestation or dissent. The silence grew so painful that I offered stumblingly to stand her lunch one day soon at an Indian restaurant in town, when we could discuss the matter. Still no response. I awoke, feeling foolish. Dreams can be most disobliging.

A week later, to test the dream, I invited my agent to lunch. She accepted. (One up on the dream.) We met at an Indian restaurant, spacious and broad-minded. Should a tear fall, it could be put down to the curry. Fortified by a poppadom and a pint of Kingfisher lager,

I said my say, proposing to withdraw on the grounds of earning her no more than – well, a rare curry lunch.

Good heavens, no! Never mind the money, think of the prestige . . . How flattering. How humiliating. But what a pleasant occasion. It even turned out that a couple of anthology fees had just been paid into my account.

The chief, recurrent difference between William Tyndale's New Testament of 1534 and that of the forty-seven scholars responsible for the Authorized Version of 1611 lies in the former's 'similitude' and the latter's 'parable'.

'All these things spake Jesus unto the people by similitudes, and without similitudes spake he nothing to them.' (Tyndale)

'All these things spake Jesus unto the multitude in parables; without a parable spake he not unto them.' (AV)

A comparison between the two versions makes the Enrights' tinkering with the Moncrieff-Mayor-Kilmartin translation of Proust's novel look like a major overhaul.

'And he spake many things unto them' – in similitudes or parables. Tyndale is a shade more direct on the cryptic incident of the unfortunate fig tree in Matthew, employing the active voice rather than the Authorized Version's passive, 'this which is done': 'If ye shall have faith and shall not doubt, ye shall not only do that which I have done to the fig tree' – namely caused it to droop and die – 'but also if ye shall say unto this mountain, take thyself away, and cast thyself into the sea, it shall be done.'

Jesus followed this with a conditional assurance: 'And whatsoever ye shall ask in prayer (if ye believe) ye shall receive it.' Faith can move mountains: it was as well that the disciples didn't take the promise literally and try it out. Perhaps Jesus's spoken parenthesis held their hand. (Brackets can emphasize as well as marginalize.) Or possibly the saying about faith and mountains was already a figure of speech.

*

Suddenly, and over a period of several days, my dictionaries let me down. Not that I was striving to write anything profound or difficult. On the contrary, it was something simple. This sounds twee, but there was nothing affected about my bewilderment and alarm over so protracted a lexical collapse. Had my spelling melted away, or my sense of alphabetical order evaporated?

I only wanted to be clear. 'My love of clarity,' Brecht wrote in his *Journals*, 'comes from the unclear way I think.'

My horoscope announces: 'As Mercury, planet of communication, links with both the Sun and Mars this week, you won't find it hard to get your message across. Your words will be short and to the point and anyone who doesn't get it must be very dumb.' So far, so good. 'But don't waste time on those of limited intelligence – you should be using this period to learn more about a subject that intrigues you and one day could earn you money.' One day: that's spoilt it.

Was tiring of Clarice Lispector's garrulous newspaper pieces, until coming on a postscript asking the kind person who translated her columns into Braille to omit one describing a visit to the Botanical Gardens, since she had 'no desire to offend eyes which cannot see'.

It is said of young Henrietta (eleven years of age) in Elizabeth Bowen's *The House in Paris* that her character 'was a mosaic of all possible kinds of prejudice'. This had come about because Henrietta was anxious to be someone, and never failed to be greatly impressed when anyone uttered a prejudice in her hearing. She 'had come to associate prejudice with identity. You could not be a someone without disliking things.'

How demeaning, that you can only be a somebody by virtue (virtue?) of disliking things, a lot of things. To achieve identity on the strength of liking things (not everything of course) – wouldn't that be more pleasing, and result in a nicer identity? 'I like Shakespeare' (or

Mozart). So does practically everybody. 'Very well, I like Fauré' (or Cavafy). A little better, but on the precious side, don't you think? And what about Wagner? Try again. 'I like smoking a pipe, I like gin and tonic, I like reading, I like cats, I like some people . . .' You don't say! What a wishy-washy nobody you must be.

June 2002: a letter from the British Council concerning that body's publications carries a postscript: 'You have a right to ask for a copy of the information we hold on you, for which we will charge a fee.' Does this mean an identity may cost you money? Not only can identities be bought and sold; it appears they can be stolen, too. We have this on the best authority, that of the Home Secretary: 'Each year, thousands of people have their identities stolen by criminals, often without their knowing about it.' (It turns out that Mr Blunkett was talking about credit card fraud.)

It appears we are better at disliking than at liking. When at last we get what we wanted, we don't want it. In *Between Security and Insecurity* (1999), the Czech writer Ivan Klíma refers to a speech he made at the Writers' Congress in 1967, regarding the evils of censorship and calling for its abolition. 'That was the main reason why I was not allowed to publish in my country for twenty years.' Others spoke out similarly and suffered similarly, or worse.

Now that the totalitarian state has crumbled, and writers and publishers enjoy freedom of expression and distribution, Klíma is appalled by what he sees around him: degrading commercial trash, violence and brutality on the television screen and in print, pornographic magazines aimed at the young. At least such material wasn't available when his children were growing up: 'For the first time ever it occurred to me that the Communist censor may have caused me plenty of worries in my life, but here was one that it spared me.' He has come to the conclusion, embarrassing in a minor degree perhaps, that the goals prized by Western civilization often bring neither satisfaction nor happiness, and 'on the contrary, in difficult situations one discovers values neglected by modern affluent societies, such as solidarity, self-sacrifice, friendship and love'.

One thinks of a traditional picture of hell, with its exquisite arrangement whereby the damned, immersed in fiery furnaces, cry out for coolness, and are then delivered into lakes of ice, where they beg for warmth. 'How comes it, then, that thou art out of hell?' 'Why, this is hell, nor am I out of it.'

On a lighter note. When young, Montaigne coveted the Order of St Michael, at that time the highest mark of honour among the French nobility, and very rarely awarded. Eventually Fortune granted it to him. But 'instead of raising me up so that I could reach it, she treated me even more graciously: she debased the Order, bringing it down to my shoulders, and lower still.'

We have never been very good at envisaging heaven. The Pope has recently been reduced to describing it *tout court* as an after-death state of being characterized by close communion with God. Given the paucity of rewards both adequate and imaginable, it is no surprise to come across an old and mean-spirited theory that the blissful souls in heaven enhanced their bliss through contemplating the miseries of those condemned in the other place.

Even without the contributions of ingeniously sadistic theologians, hell has furies enough. In a short poem of his, Marin Sorescu suggests that the worst torment of all is that the inhabitants of hell are forced to endure their pains with complete calm – they cannot avoid hearing how in paradise the just are growing fat; they are deprived of that last impeccable human right: weeping and gnashing of teeth.

> Thou madest man, he knows not why,
> He thinks he was not made to die.

*

85

While poets have succeeded better in depicting hell than in portraying heaven ('at least humanity is there, and the torments of the guilty remind us of the miseries of our life': a consideration the Romanian poet cited above would have had in mind), Chateaubriand claimed that purgatory offered literary people richer opportunities. For its inhabitants there was – uniquely – a future still undecided and in prospect, while the gradation of feelings and 'the confused sentiments of happiness and of misfortune' coming together 'could furnish the pen with touching subjects'. Purgatory sounds not unlike a remand centre.

The Abbé Mugnier, a witty, fashionable priest and acquaintance of Proust, apparently scandalized a lady by some careless remark. She exclaimed indignantly, 'In that case, M. l'Abbé, there would be no hell!' To which the Abbé replied reassuringly, 'Oh yes, Madame, there is a hell. Only there is nobody in it.' The thought – perhaps reinforced by the sight of buildings standing empty and derelict in our cities – has been repeated by a Swiss theologian said to be close to the Pope: the place exists, but a God merciful by definition couldn't sentence a soul to squat eternally in it.

We all have our professional notion of hell. There is a tale of a writer who died and was allowed to choose between going to heaven or to hell. Cannily, she asked St Peter if she might tour both regions before deciding. Led down into hell, she saw row after row of writers chained to desks, sweat running down their torsos, while demons lashed them with barbed whips. 'Dear me, let's go and look at the other place!' Ascending into heaven, she met with the sight of row after row of writers chained to desks, running with sweat, and lashed by demons wielding barbed whips. 'But this is just as dreadful as hell!' 'Oh no it isn't,' said St Peter. 'Here, your work gets published.'

April 2000, *The Oldie* has a cartoon of more general import. In hell, a senior devil brings a novice up to date: 'We don't call them "the damned" any more – we call them customers.'

*

Relativities. A charitable appeal bears the word 'TORTURE!' stamped askew on the cover. We know what that forebodes. We have read the reports and looked at the pictures before. Still, we open it. It comes from an organization set up to help sufferers from tinnitus.

Having complained of frantic novels, sickly and stupid German tragedies, idle and extravagant stories in verse, and the degrading thirst after outrageous stimulation (a feast for any Minister of Culture!), Wordsworth concluded with a muted but indispensable flourish of trumpets: 'Reflecting upon the magnitude of the general evil, I should be oppressed with no dishonourable melancholy, had I not a deep impression of certain inherent and indestructible qualities of the human mind . . .'

In *The Uses of Literacy* (1957), dealing with 'changes in working-class culture during the last thirty or forty years . . . with special reference to publications and entertainment', Richard Hoggart quoted this last passage – an old consolation that many of my generation invoked scores of times in private thought. Largely Hoggart had in mind the people he grew up among. That's ancient history. How much longer can this faith, this 'comfort serves in a whirlwind', survive in our technologically speeded-up age?

If it can truly be said to survive. For an account of electronic entertainment and computer role-playing games, see John Sutherland in the *London Review of Books*, 29 July 1999 (or, if you have the courage, read the book he is reviewing). It appears that virtual reality (VR), where a little imagination goes a long way, promises to overtake and stifle real life (RL), where a lot of imagination goes a little way.

The changes between Hoggart's time and the present have been far greater than those between Wordsworth's time and Hoggart's. Wordsworth talked of 'outrageous stimulation'; more temperately, understandably loath to sound portentous, Hoggart spoke of 'invitations to a candy-floss world'. These days, nothing but mumbled demurrals.

'And God saw every thing that he had made, and, behold, it was very good.' By and large, the media have been busy correcting this hasty judgement.

An *Oldie* cartoon. Elderly wife scolds elderly husband: 'I would never have agreed to getting this computer if I'd known you were going to spend morning, noon and night on it! What on earth are you doing, that's so important?' Husband: 'Trying to turn it on.'

Our grandchildren were at home with computers before they could tie their shoelaces. Yet they go on reading books, quite naturally, carrying them with them wherever they go. Ah, the pessimist will say, they can't carry computers with them – yet. But I have no desire to display any honourable or dishonourable melancholy, or even feel it. A measure of anxiety is another matter, also quite natural.

Literal translation of answer in French baccalaureate examination: 'Jacques Prévert wrote *Paroles* because he was going out at night and had things to say.'

> It is well known or at least believed
> That belief is our very backbone
> A human property or privilege or right or duty
> I have believed my share or more in my time
> I have believed this and that
> And have not believed (which is also belief)
> That and this
> But now I have somehow spurned the privilege
> Relinquished the right and shirked the duty
> Perhaps there is simply too much belief in the world
> Though I strive to remain polite on the point

For it is a comfort no doubt to believe or (a form of belief)
Not to.
A thing had better be this or that
To me it is this and that and other things besides
I shall lose my citizenship, my passport will refuse
To recognize me
The baker does not deign to sell me a loaf
Unless I avouch my faith in the staff of life
The vintner insists I should trust in vintages
The newsagent withholds the daily paper
Till I promise faithfully to read the headlines
With intent to believe

But who or whom have I the honour of addressing
I don't believe I know you

           ('Beyond belief', believed to be after J. Prévert)

Writing about his early years in *A Double Thread*, and about wanting the best of both worlds, John Gross observes that the word 'ambiguity' took on blessedness: 'the fact that so many things contained their opposite was on the whole a comfort'. In one's later years too, and maybe more so. Sweet things are bad for you, sugar is good for you. Pain is a sign that something's wrong, feeling pain shows you are still alive. Staying indoors saves money but enfeebles you, going out is invigorating but you may be mugged. Smoking damages health, but you don't have much health to damage. Ambiguity keeps your mind open and your mouth shut. Which is – ambiguous, but on the whole not unhelpful. 'Without contraries is no progression.'

Musical beds. The soap operas don't go in for ambiguities, or for marriage (there just isn't time for it). As it is, practically every character of one sex has slept with every character of the other.

Grant Mitchell, of *EastEnders*, was called on to bed both his mother-in-law and his sister-in-law. What to do? Introduce new characters, or – memories are short – start all over again from scratch. VR or RL?

Herodotus was much impressed by the marriage mart, a custom followed by the Babylonians. At a public gathering, rich men in need of wives bid for the prettiest girls, the auctioneer beginning with the best-looking and continuing down the scale. Then came the turn of the plainest girls: the auctioneer asked who would take each of them along with the smallest sum of money. The money came from the sale of the beauties, who in this way 'provided dowries for their ugly or misshapen sisters'.

Unfortunately this 'admirable practice' had fallen into disuse at the time of writing, and the Babylonians resorted to another scheme: the prostitution of all girls of the poverty-stricken lower classes.

Hardly less ingenious than their marriage mart, Herodotus considered, was the Babylonians' method of coping with health problems. And of greater interest to us, given the finances of the NHS and the reduction of worn-out GPs to split-second diagnosis and routine prescription. The Babylonians had no doctors, and simply stationed their sick in the streets, where those coming along would stop, discuss whatever ailment it was, and suggest measures which they, their relatives or friends, had found beneficial. Nobody was allowed to sidle past in silence; all had to stop and carry out their civic duty. A democratic, community medicine, free from the delays and expense of bureaucracy.

There was trouble between the Perinthians and the Paeonians. An oracle told the Paeonians that once they had come face to face with the Perinthians, if the latter called on them by name they should attack, but otherwise withdraw. When the two armies met, a challenge was issued and three champions from each side met in single combat: man against man, horse against horse, and dog against dog. Seeing that their champions were gaining the upper hand in this curtain-raiser, the Perinthians shouted out the cry of triumph, *Io Paean*. Whereupon the Paeonians, following the oracle's advice, fell on them at once and won a great victory.

The ancients had a proper respect for language, including the power of puns. (The derivation of 'pun' is uncertain, but it seems unrelated to 'pundit'.) Puns were of immense value to the oracles: if an oracle proved wrong in one interpretation, another interpretation could show how right it was. Oracles weren't meant to be simple and straightforward; if they were, there wouldn't be anything *divine* about them. As it was, they stayed in business.

Quite possibly the oracles went in for anagrams, too. At the time when Alexander the Great was thinking of abandoning the siege of Tyre, he dreamt that he saw a satyr dancing round him. This he interpreted as an omen since the Greek for 'satyr' could be turned into the words 'Tyre is yours'. And the next day Tyre was his. Tony Augarde (*Oxford Guide to Word Games*) also mentions the Frenchman, André Pujam, who discovered that his name could be read as 'pendu à Riom'. Believing that anagrams foretold things to come, he committed a murder and was duly hanged at Riom, in Auvergne. So how should we interpret the Driver and Vehicle Licensing Agency's anagram mentioned earlier: 'Untied Kingdom'?

It appears that Cubby Broccoli, producer of James Bond films, when asked why he continued working into his eighties, replied: 'If I didn't, I would turn into a vegetable.'

'A work of wonderful bad taste that is part cannibalistic sex and part revenge farce . . . What the play is actually about is anybody's guess, but it's so gut-wrenchingly funny that it doesn't really matter.' Two days later the same critic hailed a play featuring Jesus as a Texan homosexual whose relationship with Judas turns sour; his lover betrays him with a kiss. The play – called (a gift!) *Corpus Christi* – is 'perfect for a time in which gay bars can be bombed'. And the critic jeers at 'the knee-jerk reactions of self-appointed moral guardians'.

Knee-jerks: you are reactionary, I am responsive.

The reflection above is just one example of what someone in the same 'paper of record', reviewing (quite amiably) this book's predecessor, referred to as 'old-fartism'. I fear my flatulence hasn't subsided since.

The language of criticism . . . Of a new novel: 'Phrases, anecdotes and atmosphere roll off the page with the ease and sublime, scary grace of drunken eels.' And what the devil does this signify, said of another book?: 'Although I never want to read this novel again, I wouldn't hesitate to recommend it to a jaundiced reader.' Are there special schools teaching how to express putative judgements in dazzling tropes, outré allusions and generally extravagant prose? 'XY writes like a dream. Almost literally.' One is so grateful for the 'almost' that one almost supposes one knows what is meant. A fourth novel elicits a weird but maybe apt token of praise: 'As fresh as a new gun wound.'

The Man Without Qualities points towards a partial explanation of the phenomenon in its early stages. All those epithets distinguished men have applied to other distinguished men (Shakespeare's 'wealth of imagination', Goethe's 'universality', and so on) outlive their recipients and hang about in their hundreds. They have to be put to use, and hence you hear every fashionable writer (not to say tennis player) described as 'great', 'richly imaginative', 'all-embracing', etc. Eventually these epithets wear thin from excessive handling, and a new vocabulary is sought out.

*

How is it one acquires an unwarranted reputation for large-scale philanthropy? A letter from a mission school in Malawi, neatly handwritten, explains that by the grace of God they have discovered my name and address, and God has led them to ask for £1,000. Two days later another letter arrives, even more handsomely penned, with only one mistake ('recieve'), from Gladys, a student nurse in Uganda, whose parents perished recently in a boat disaster on Lake Victoria, asking for a mere £200 towards her school dues. 'It is a blessing from God that I have been able to write to you.' An omniscient God really ought to be better informed on the subject of my finances. I send Gladys a little something, partly because of a cheery nurse of the same name at St George's Hospital.

'Praise the Lord for getting your Address!' A letter from Kampala written – ostensibly written – by a young woman whose misfortunes do not bear repetition. Enclosed is a photocopy of a barely literate communication from a firm of Advocates and Solicitors respecting 216 dollars US in ground rent owed to 'the land lord on which you are residing', and informing the young woman that she has 45 days to pay this debt 'or else you will face and bear the consequences without any regrets'. The communication ends: 'No further Notice will be issued to you, so stand dully warned.'

Saw – was seen by – brilliant, witty surgeon at St George's. 'So you're a writer?' (Better than being a waiter?) To keep my end up, I mentioned the *Oxford Book of Death*. 'Every doctor should have a copy, eh?' he (who obviously didn't) quipped. 'And every patient,' I muttered. He gave me an appointment for an endoscopy ('Upper GI') on the very next day at 1 p.m. I couldn't believe it.

The next day I fast obediently and prepare spiritually (well, mentally) for the examination, with the help of a jaunty pamphlet. ('The back of your throat may feel sore for the rest of the day. You may also feel a little bloated if some of the air has remained in your stomach. Both these discomforts will pass.') Around 10 a.m. the surgeon's secretary phones to explain, a little sheepishly, that as it happens the Endoscopy Unit is closed for maintenance work all day, and the appointment has to be deferred *sine die*. I can believe it.

Sine die? No such luck. The appointment was deferred by a mere week. I'd better believe it. Fasted from midnight (no great sacrifice). Then had to hang about, to the muted drone of anodyne pop music, for four hours. The procedure itself was surprisingly discomfort-free. Throat sprayed with something tasting of banana soaked in acid. The sedative injection worked like a dream, a dreamless one. Then a cup of tea and a couple of biscuits. I couldn't believe it. No fault of the endoscopy that it couldn't reveal the cause of my anaemia. Related to rheumatoid arthritis, our GP and I agreed. Just another consequence of officiousness on the part of the immune system, the white blood cells mistaking the red for noxious raiders and shooting them down.

Several years back, a scientific study concluded that a stag experiences severe stress when hunted. A supporter of stag-hunting promptly claimed that another scientific study, in progress, would prove the opposite: a hunted stag does not experience stress.

This new study has just been published. It maintains that the stress levels of a hunted stag are no greater than those of a racehorse engaged in long courses such as the Grand National (not much of an endorsement), and that the deer are not pushed far beyond their physiological limits. (No mention of their emotional limits.)

How stress levels are measured or physiological limits determined is not divulged. Perhaps some variety of tachograph or black box is attached to a test animal who is then chased across the countryside for a few hours. Clearly imagination and common sense are not consulted. Next we shall hear that stags, like other animals, positively enjoy being hunted – you can tell by the light in their eyes and the grin on their faces.

*

'And God said unto them, Be fruitful, and multiply, and replenish the earth, and subdue it: and have dominion over the fish of the sea, and over the fowl of the air, and over every living thing that moveth upon the earth.' And multiply they did, and had dominion.

At first, a line of flame and smoke cloud in the distance. Next, closer to, a mound of legs, sticking up in the air, wreathed in wispy smoke. Then, very close, clearly visible, piles of dead animals smouldering or waiting to be burnt or buried. We move from the first book of the Bible to the last. 'There arose a smoke out of the pit, as the smoke of a great furnace; and the sun and the air were darkened.' And, a sore point: 'The merchants of the earth shall weep and mourn over her; for no man buyeth their merchandise any more.'

A fourteen-day-old calf is found alive, next to its dead mother, under a pile of slaughtered cows. Phoenix – as her perspicacious owners now call her – is eminently photogenic and features widely and repeatedly in the media. The Ministry of Agriculture attributes the 'fuss' about Phoenix to 'hideous sentimentality'. None the less, shortly afterwards, the policy of slaughter is modified, and the calf is spared – 'saved by a change of heart', one newspaper says (doing the spin-doctors' work for them), as if the Ministry had a heart. The Minister himself, however, insists that the change or 'refinement' of policy has been made in accord with scientific advice, not sentiment.

'Hideous sentimentality'! The story of Phoenix is the only thing about the foot-and-mouth outbreak not to be hideous. 'Sentimentality' may seem a handy way of discounting some irksome little inconvenience – a sad reflection on our society, if so – but the Ministry really should watch its words. Phoenix has become a symbol, and governments do well to show a proper respect for symbols.

Now a pig unhelpfully called Porky is in peril. The pet of a couple of

pensioners, who describe him as a 'polite old gentleman' disinclined
to consort with farm animals, he too has his picture in the papers:
pot-bellied, eighteen stone in weight, ten years of age, 'less visually
appealing' than Phoenix, and less prone to arouse hideous
sentimentality. The 'refinement' of policy doesn't seem to favour
Porky; there must have been quite a few gentlemanly or ladylike
creatures among the eight million or so already slaughtered.
Lawyers have been engaged to plead for his life. Lawyers and
symbols don't go well together. Moreover, we can have too much of
a good thing. One symbol good, two symbols bad.

We old gents in Vernon Ward compliment the nurses at every turn
– their skill, their kindness, their looks – and behave with the utmost
decorum. But we can't compete with the likes of this young doctor:
Dr Leal by name, so a nurse vouchsafes, one of those crowding
excitedly around him. Later, calm (or boredom) having returned to
the ward, I discover that his name is Dr Neil B.

The speech of many doctors is as indecipherable as their
handwriting. Not so with Dr B., who is telling the patient in the bed
opposite mine that he had been terminally ill – the poor man,
obviously frail, looks mildly confused: could he have been terminally
ill without actually dying? – but they had saved him then, and they
will save him now, just as long as he does exactly what he is told. So
masterful! The patient smiles indeterminately: silence seems his best
bet. 'Let me know the number of my days: that I may be certified
how long I have to live' – Dr B. would come out with the answer, to
the nearest hour, at the drop of a stethoscope.

My turn comes, and he fixes his unwavering gaze on my decrepit
person. I search desperately for something innocuous, totally
unprovocative, to say, and nearly come out with 'Shall I be around
for Christmas?', inadvertently recalling the words, a week before he
died, of a young friend, a bearded teacher of English in Tokyo,
alluding to a famous department store: 'Takashimaya will damned

well have to find another Father Christmas this year.' Luckily, Dr B. gets in first with a poetic reference to 'a carpet of tumours' excised the previous day, and follows up by predicating with some gusto an untoward connection between my tobacco pipe and the state of my bladder.

A month later I am recalled to hospital. X-rays taken as I was leaving on the previous occasion have shown a tumour lurking uncomfortably near my remaining kidney. I gather circuitously that the ureter may have to be reinforced with a plastic tube. (Ureter, not urethra.) Sounds nasty. Once again I pull out a large old envelope marked 'Important Papers', containing my will, birth certificate, marriage certificate, national insurance and health service numbers, share certificates relating to a small bankrupt publishing house (kept as a souvenir), an Equitable Life policy, a testimonial from F. R. Leavis dated 1946, and a letter from L. C. Knights regretting that he couldn't act as a referee since my published work mostly concerned German literature, a subject with which he was less than intimate – and place it conspicuously in the centre of my desk.

Fully armed, the cystoscope advances along the well-worn thoroughfare into the bladder (not that I am aware of this, being under general anaesthetic), but can find no trace of a tumour. What showed up on the photograph must have been old scarring, Dr B. admits testily, as the great consultant and his entourage sweep through the ward. Dr B. gives the impression of having disclosed what ought to have been left unsaid. I attempt an emollient joke about a sense of tumour. But the doctor has vanished.

Patients who crack jokes, even jokes meant to make life just a little easier for their medics, are not welcome in the NHS, which is no laughing matter. A solemn, humble and dutiful demeanour is advisable at all times. (This rule excludes dealings with nurses, who might be moved to press the panic button.)

*

Mad for most of his life, the great philosopher had even so caused a great stir. Then, in Turin, recovering from a plethora of aphorisms, he ran into the street and threw his arms around the neck of an old cart-horse being flogged by its driver. This caused a small public stir in the piazza. A measure of sanity was renewed in him, along with gentleness, compassion and a childlike sweetness. This spelt the end of his career as a great philosopher.

'Ah! gentle, fleeting, wav'ring sprite, friend and associate of this clay!' The soul, not accounted for at all convincingly in encyclopae-dias ('the ultimate identity of a person': like a passport or identity card?), maltreated in uncouth idioms (in French, *l'âme*: the hollow bubble at the bottom of a wine bottle), a flimsy shade among giant genes, though not so uncommon in the scattered metaphors of ancient poets and even a few moderns. Whatever it is that isn't the body, although the one is the best picture of the other; the guest of the body (not always to its advantage or the body's); a nightingale's soul is poured forth abroad; in age, if you are lucky, clapping hands and singing; a numberless infinity of them; even housemaids used to have them, albeit damp.

Otherwise, largely undefined, address unknown, denied yet not wholly dispensable. Immortal it must be: just consider all the things that would have killed the soul stone-dead if it hadn't been. Yet if immortal, to what extent can it be a true friend and equal associate of our distinctly mortal part? What then, if at all, can it be? Not its sundry sometimes synonyms. Hardly the mind, which reasons: Not me, thank you, better things to be thought; even less the brain, doing its sums, brisk in workplace, in profit and loss, interned in the Internet. (And not the self, whose hatefulness we have noted.) A rather dismal concept on the whole, the soul, you need to die to know for certain whether or not it lives.

Robert Musil remarked, the young cannot pronounce the word without laughing (they have other, less laughable concerns); the middle-aged fight shy of it (perhaps it hints at hitherto unrecognized misdemeanours and shames resisted). It is decidedly a word for the elderly, who have nothing further to lose, who might conceivably (inconceivably) have something to gain, who may even prefer to talk to themselves. Or ask, like the soldier on the eve of battle: Please, God, if there is a God, save my soul, if I have a soul.

'Do you have a soul? This question, which may be philosophical, theological, or simply misguided in nature, has a particular relevance for our time. In the wake of psychiatric medicines, aerobics, and media zapping, does the soul still exist?' Julia Kristeva's *New Maladies of the Soul* starts off promisingly – in this context one can condone, even welcome, the shifty word 'relevance', and perhaps satisfy oneself for the nonce with the supposition that aerobics feature here as a popular activity exclusively and zealously concerned with the flesh – but very soon the book slides into what its English translator almost apologetically describes as a 'highly technical psychoanalytic and semiological terminology'. Bang goes the soul.

'How can *a soul* be a merchant? What relation to an immortal being have the price of linseed, the fall of butter, the tare on tallow, the brokerage on hemp? Can an undying creature debit "petty expenses" and charge for "carriage paid"?' Thus Walter Bagehot, many-sided journalist and editor of *The Economist* (1860–77) in serio-comic vein. 'The soul ties its shoes; the mind washes its hands in a basin. All is incongruous.' An awkward customer, the soul.

Professor Lupin, specialist in Defence Against the Dark Arts in *Harry Potter and the Prisoner of Azkaban*, offers a neat account: 'You can exist without your soul, you know, as long as your brain and heart are still working. But you'll have no sense of self any more, no memory, no . . . anything. You'll just – exist. As an empty shell.' Wisdom out of the mouth of a children's book. To it one might add a question asked in Karl Čapek's *R.U.R.*: 'Do you think that the soul first shows itself by a gnashing of teeth?' A feasible start – after those happy, early days, as Henry Vaughan wrote,

> Before I understood this place
> Appointed for my second race,
> Or taught my soul to fancy aught
> But a white, celestial thought.

'Before I understood this place.' A new year's wish: that one could read the newspaper without wanting to throw up. Once it was the best that was known and thought in the world that our attention seized on, however fumblingly. Now – and so deftly – it's the worst that is done in the world.

If we didn't do such dreadful things, we would have a better opinion of ourselves. If we had a better opinion of ourselves, we wouldn't do such dreadful things.

That splinter of ice in the writer's heart, remarked on by Graham Greene – in old age it melts into tears.

The 'scholarship boy' (of old, but perhaps still now): 'He has been equipped for hurdle-jumping; so he merely thinks of getting on, but somehow not in the world's way . . . He has left his class, at least in spirit, by being in certain ways unusual; and he is still unusual in another class, too tense and overwound': Richard Hoggart.

Permanently in irksome debt, morally speaking, to his origins, the scholarship boy doesn't have to do well, he has to do brilliantly, making sure to become a top professor at Oxford or Cambridge, one of the best writers around, a great inventor, a celebrated surgeon, a senior politician (not that he thinks much of politicians).

He must be offered a peerage (which naturally he will decline), and above all he needs to make a lot of money – not because he reveres money, for he certainly doesn't, but because it is the objective proof of success, and he can give it to his parents (who are long since dead). In short, he can never do sufficiently well, never be 'usual' enough.

(I had never suggested to my mother that she should read anything of mine, nor had she shown any interest in that disreputable side of my life. But when *The Terrible Shears* came out in 1975, I proposed tentatively that she might care to take a quick look through the book since it was about our family way back in the twenties and thirties. My mother was now in her eighty-fifth year. She took the book, grimacing faintly as if it might blow up in her face. Some days later she handed the book back, a stiff, displeased look on her face, a look I hadn't seen for a long time. I had broken an unspoken but fundamental rule: never speak of personal matters, keep yourself to yourself. Eventually she said: 'You have a good memory': which wasn't meant as praise. Still, I was getting off lightly. 'It *is* dedicated to you,' I mumbled. 'See?' This placated her somewhat, I think, for she sighed gently and accepted the book.)

There's something very satisfying about Montaigne's reports on the doings of Fortune, especially if one doesn't expect to get far on merit alone. That whimsical goddess cares naught for the pains of hurdle-jumping, or effortfully making good, or justifying oneself. Take Jason Phereus, given up by his doctors because of a tumour on his breast, who rushed recklessly into battle and was pierced through the body at exactly the right spot, lancing the tumour and thus saving his life. Or the city wall of Arona mined by Captain Renzo: blown into the air, the wall fell back on to its foundations settling all in one piece, and leaving the besieged citizens alive and no worse off than they had been. And the story of the painter, Protogenes, who had almost finished a portrait of an exhausted dog, but couldn't get its foaming slaver right. Exasperated, he threw a sponge at it saturated with various paints, intending to blot everything out. Guided by Fortune, the sponge landed on the dog's mouth and achieved the very effect Protogenes had been striving after.

All this without any scholarships being required.

This week's horoscope: 'You are straining at the leash and eager to get started. But what on and for what purpose?' You tell me, you're the expert. Solar and lunar activity in Scorpio, you say, will give me all the get-up-and-go I need. But still no indication of where to go, apart from the suggestion that I could do worse than invest in a last-minute holiday. Last-minute? Horoscopes never fail to impress, in one way or another. And since they have to accommodate twelve signs and untold thousands of readers, they can't be too specific and they have to be mercifully short. Twinkle, twinkle, little star.

Inflation in academe! Robert Nisbet records the mushrooming titles of a political scientist holding offices at two universities: Allison W. Scott Distinguished Service Research Professor and Director of the Miriam Angston Butler Institute for Political Analysis at the University of Renown (obviously) *and* Elmer Crittenden Distinguished Professor and Director of the Mark J. Smith Center for the Study of Political Dynamics at Urban University Graduate Center. When the gentleman retired from these universities, 'Emeritus' was added to each title. Then he took a post at a third university, which furnished him with a titled chair and an institute directorship. 'It is said that editors and typesetters cringed when articles were submitted by this political scientist, for he was meticulous about title and did not take kindly to omission of a word.'

On the wrapper of *Prejudices: A Philosophical Dictionary*, Robert Nisbet is described as Albert Schweitzer Professor of the Humanities, Emeritus, Columbia University. ('For the present, the lamented

state of the humanities,' says the professor, 'brings to mind
Nietzsche's statement, "When you see something slipping, push it."')
Is there really a University of Renown? Nisbet may have altered
names and titles to fend off costly litigation and the possible
expunction of his current Emeritus.

'Take but degree away, untune that string, and hark! What discord
follows.' The more there is of something, whatever it may be, the
more words, adjectives and epithets are needed to distinguish
between the indistinguishable.

There used to be an expression, 'conspicuous consumption'. This
has disappeared, what it represents having become normal and
therefore no longer conspicuous.

A solemnly worded catalogue arrives, offering (among much else)
a hand-held satellite system that will tell you where you are on the
planet to within fifty metres (as they say, you can never find a
policeman when you want one); a revolutionary cushion which helps
you get up from a seated position and also helps you get down to a
seated position (six settings adjustable to your weight); a neck
massager for use in the car ('like having a personal masseur with you
on every trip': NB, not for use while driving); Paul McKenna's
hypnotherapy tapes, to help you give up smoking, lose weight,
eliminate stress, sleep better (also not to be used while driving); a
Life Hammer for slicing seat-belts and smashing windows in the
event of a car crash; a Shower Companion which pipes in radio
programmes and features a digital voice memo function to record
any important thoughts you may have while soaping yourself; a
variety of devices to chase off moles, cats and mice by emitting
powerful (though harmless) blasts of ultrasonic sound; 'Nature's
answer to lost virility': a combination of four herbs found in the
Amazon rain forest, 'which are traditionally believed to be
supportive of male sexual organs and systems'; Wonder Shape

Breast Enhancers (pair), silicone gel in a cell, whereby you can bring about, without recourse to implants or surgery, either increased fullness of bust or of cleavage or both simultaneously.

A subsequent catalogue, 'Bright Ideas for Christmas', more relaxed in manner, presents a Celestial Ball programmed to answer 'the most pressing questions about living and loving in the new millennium' (you just prod it, whereupon thunderclaps and heavenly harps are heard, followed by the Voice of the Future solemnly pronouncing your destiny); a mask, suitable for adults or children, which makes you look like an alien, while an Alien Voice Simulator makes you sound like one; a moulded latex Bog Monster for attachment to the underside of a lavatory seat, ready to rear up 'in all its hideous glory' when the seat is lifted; and, for those moments when pressure in the office gets too much, an Executive Stress Shooter empowering you to fire harmless soft foam rings at a hyperactive phone, irritating colleagues or a stuffy MD, accompanied by flashing lights and arcade-style sound effects (there is no NB warning against use by employees desiring to keep their jobs or Christmas bonuses).

There'll always be something for the man or woman who has everything – except a brain.

Haven't come across 'miniscule' or 'dessicated' for ages, which shows that battles can still be won (or drawn). 'Guttural' (from Latin *guttur*, throat) is lost to us, I fear, supplanted by 'gutteral', probably inspired by the noise of water going down the drain ('gutter' from Latin *gutta*, drop), and perhaps, though less common, 'idiosyncrasy' replaced by 'idiosyncracy'. Rife is the faulty grammar of 'between you and I' and the newspaper headline 'Work comes second for Tony and I'; rather touching, though: the speaker or writer knows that politeness requires one to put oneself last, but fails to notice that 'I' (now banished to the end of the phrase) ought to be 'me'. He or she would never say or write 'between I and you'. A pamphlet of devotional verses brought by the postman includes this stanza:

> A rainbow, says our gracious God,
> when it glows across the sky,
> just reaffirms a Covenant
> that's made 'twixt you and I.

At least God has the excuse that, while he didn't need to be polite but was, he did need to rhyme.

'Whom' lies mortally wounded ('Argentina, who England will face in their second group match . . .': *The Times*), but may be called back to life when 'who' sounds blatantly offbeat, as in 'To who it concerns', while the homophonic accident, 'the man whose lost his job', is rare as yet (unlike that all too common 'your' for 'you're').

On the pronunciation front, 'h*a*rass' has surrendered to 'har*a*ss', the word more frequently heard on television than any other: it would appear that these days practically everyone is being harassed by someone or something. Matthew Arnold had no doubt where the stress should lie:

> Too fast we live, too much are tried,
> Too harassed to attain
> Wordsworth's sweet calm, or Goethe's wide
> And luminous view to gain.

But Arnold was a poet, and hence unacknowledged as a legislator.

The ousting of 'miniscule' – I spoke too soon. A review in *The Times* (no less) of Derwent May's *Critical Times: The History of the Times Literary Supplement* (no less) alludes to the 'miniscule payment' to contributors of ten pence per word (no less?). (Later on, mention is made of a debate in the correspondence columns regarding 'the morality of Nabakov' *sic*.)

*

A third leader in *The Times* informs us that 'the first line of *The Waste Land* – "April is the cruellest month" – is probably more quoted than Keats's sugary "Oh, to be in England/ Now that April's there."' And there were we, thinking that this home thought from abroad (more hideous sentimentality?) was Browning's.

And the same paper, a fortnight later, draws a comparison between Helmut Kohl, the German Chancellor, and Hardy's Mayor of Casterbridge, favouring the latter as a victim of merely a single act of folly, 'who in a moment of drunken madness fells his wife'. Nothing so brutal: in the novel he merely sells her to a sailor.

Alluding to the title of Thomas Wolfe's novel, a writer in the *Times Literary Supplement* quoted the pertinent line from *Lycidas* as 'Look homeward, Angel, now, and melt in truth.' A striking image: truth as both harsh solvent and gentle softener. But Milton's words were 'melt in ruth'. An American reader spotted the slip: he remembered the line, he said, because he was courting a girl called Ruth when the novel came out, and he thought that Milton's advice made good sense.

A couple of months later, the same periodical referred to the American poet, Edna St Vincent Millais. No correction forthcoming. (Nag, nag, nag.)

Ultrasound scan. Sturdy woman doctor, Chinese, is digging urgently into my left side. 'You do know,' I venture timorously, 'that my left kidney has been removed?' 'Oh,' says she, 'so that's why I couldn't find it! They might have told me.'

As our GP taps me here and there with her little hammer, as she gently twists my lower limbs, and then makes out a hospital chit for hip X-rays, I am tempted to quote Coleridge: 'It is a small thing that the patient knows of his own state; yet some things he *does* know better than his physician.' I don't, of course. She is a sensitive, solicitous, determined young woman, never hesitating to track down and tackle some grand cloistered consultant, and I don't wish to be a petulant old man whose 'moi' is playing up. I muse silently on Montaigne's saying, that he would rather be an expert on himself than on Cicero. (There's a sturdy, prepossessing 'moi' for all to see.)

A few days later and the X-rays prove unnecessary, the pains and disability having moved to other joints. Also I was caught up in more sombre thoughts. Montaigne noted that 'he who recalls the ills he has endured, those that have threatened him, the trifling incidents which have moved him from one state to another, is prepared thereby for future mutations and the recognition of his condition'.

One of the wisdoms we gain from experience lies in recalling – a singularly taxing procedure – how often we have been wrong in our judgements. The doctor would have been justified in counter-claiming that the patient knows one or two little things, the physician many big ones. But she belongs to that rare breed who do not 'act the professor' by talking too much – or by saying nothing. Once, in hospital for a routine check-up, I came to in a ward with a catheter between my legs. No one told me why or what, though an Indian lady of tragic mien in a long black robe, gliding past, murmured that she was sorry. (I would have supposed I was hallucinating except that my wife was there and vouched for the incident.) The next morning a senior doctor made the rounds, chatting with everybody in the ward but me. 'Hey, aren't you going to spare me a word?' I asked as he was leaving. He halted briefly: 'Good morning.' I imagine I was the sole property of a surgeon (it turned out that he had removed a bladder tumour) who was engaged elsewhere. With the help of brisk, kindly nurses I made a reasonably rapid recovery.

An old grey-faced man a few beds away, in a dreadful state, couldn't or wouldn't say a word to his wordless wife when she visited, a trial to the nurses hunting for the bloodstained pyjama trousers he had hidden, he moaned throughout the night.

A tall black orderly on the ward, standing upright, silent, staring into space, as if he had just arrived from a far-off country, speaking to no one, no one speaking to him, he appeared to have no duties.

Seen early one morning, the orderly, upright, stock-still, expressionless, hugging the sick old man, quiet now, close to his chest, not a word passing between them. So that was what he was there for.

'I remember the ludicrous effect produced on my mind by the first sentence of an autobiography, which, happily for the writer, was as meagre in incident as it is well possible for the life of an individual to be – "The *eventful* life which I am about to record . . .'": Coleridge speaking. I remember an autobiography offered to Chatto and the covering letter in which the writer, more modest perhaps, conjectured that an account of his uneventful life would appeal to those many readers to whom, also, nothing out of the ordinary had ever happened. This singular preamble captured my errant attention and, pushing aside yet another commentary on the work of Virginia Woolf, I took up the manuscript. The author was right about his life. Its one outstanding event was an embarrassing outbreak of acne during adolescence, to which, perhaps reluctantly, he felt honour-bound to devote several pages. Sadly – for it is not often that a manuscript chimes with its author's description of it – we could not convince ourselves that a sufficient market existed for the book, whether among those interested in acne or those interested in the total absence of interest.

Is your life meagre in incidents? Are you deficient in disaster? Do you crave a thrilling mission? Then 'Immerse yourself in a great disaster', or embark on an 'Undersea mission that could turn you into a wreck'. A reviewer of two computer games involving the *Titanic* awards the first a feelgood factor of nine out of ten and the second seven out of ten. So that's what 'feelgood' signifies – a demotic euphemism for 'decadent' befitting our day and age.

'Praise the lord Jesus for the opportunity of writing to you.' Another letter from Uganda, in another beautifully neat hand. Esther is a girl of eighteen, with five siblings under the age of thirteen. Her father is dead of AIDS, and her mother is seriously ill with the disease. She must therefore prepare herself to take care of the other children, and wishes to complete her teacher-training course. 'When I get my certificate, chances of getting a job employment are at times bright.' I guess I'll send a small sum, nothing like the £248 she requires. If you are given something to write about, you should think of paying for it once in a while.

A press report now has it that in many cases this is a scam and the girls never see the money. At least, unlike well-established domestic charities, they don't send ballpoint pens 'to help you reply quickly' or make changes to your will. By coincidence, my current horoscope warns me against giving time or money to causes I know little about or people I cannot be sure are truly deserving. 'This is not selfish, it's sensible.'

(A year later Esther writes again, rather more brusquely: 'Dear Enright . . .' She has been advised by the chief education officer to enrol in a computer training course for six months, which costs £150. 'I will be very grateful when you sponsor me.' What next? A doctorate in economics, training as a neurosurgeon?)

The lovely illusions that attend our days! For long I had believed the brand name of Marks & Spencer's clothing to be St Martin, after the fourth-century soldier who divided his cloak with a naked beggar, and became Bishop of Tours. Hence, I assumed, a discreet hint that cast-off trousers, shirts or coats should be donated to

Oxfam. (The beggar turned out to be Christ.) Eventually it was borne in on me that the M&S saint was Michael, 'of celestial armies prince' who on Judgement Day weighs the souls of the risen dead in his scales. The childish disillusions that ensue!

We still need hyphens, preferably in the right places. In *The New Fowler's Modern English Usage*, R. W. Burchfield observes that there is a world of difference between 'thirty-odd people' and 'thirty odd people', and lists such fallacious (if entertaining) end-of-line breaks as 'berib-boned', 'pain-staking' and 'fru-ity'. Typesetters are not always punctilious in this respect, while the proliferation of pushy computers has compounded the confusion.

A letter to *The Times* of 25 August 1999 cited 'pronoun-cement' appearing in that paper, while another letter of the same date awarded the prize for ghoulish ineptitude to 'brains-canner'. Subsequent correspondents, however, praised their computers for showing initiative in the shape of 'bed-raggled' and for adding usefully to our word-hoard with 'not-ables', a neologism so well defining 'a class of persons to be found occupying senior positions in many organizations'. (There is no respectable way of hyphenating this word: 'no-tables' is cryptic and 'nota-bles' inscrutable.)

On the front page of *The Times*, 11 December 1999, I spotted a weird reference to Madeleine Albright and Robin Cook meeting in 'a Georget-own restaurant' in Washington. Some of my favourite perversions, 'the-rapist', 'men-swear', 'mans-laughter', crop up in John Murray's *A Gentleman Publisher's Commonplace Book*, along with 'not-iced' (another word unamenable to hyphenation), 'to-wed', 'male-factor' (if you must hyphenate, the *Oxford Minidictionary of Spelling* can only suggest 'mal-efactor'), and the demythologizing, down-to-earth 'leg-end of King Arthur's Table'.

Professor Roy Harris has drawn the attention of *The Times* to its 'alarming report concerning the "hot dog-munching sports fans" who allegedly fill baseball parks in the US'. More mysteriously poignant, a misplaced hyphen in an old *Sunday Times* magazine has inspired a poem by Charles Boyle, 'Literals':

Ask them why so sad
the streets-weepers here
in the dun garb of the borough cleansing department . . .

(Here, 'dun' is neither Dr Johnson's low epithet nor the dictionary's '*poet*', but is defined in another sense as 'dull greyish brown', factual and rather dull, though tinged with melancholy by the context. Karl Kraus remarked that the more closely one looks at a word, the further back it points into its own history.)

The wretchedness of the human condition, says Montaigne, means that we have less to enjoy than to avoid, that extreme sensual delight touches us less than the lightest of pains. (Once a generally received or at least professed opinion: 'For the world, I count it not an inn, but an hospital': Sir Thomas Browne.) Being well means not being ill. For instance, 'The appetite which transports us in our relations with women seeks only to dispel the pain caused by ardent and frenzied desire; it aims only to assuage desire and bring us to rest and repose, freed from that fever.' (Tell that to the entertainment industry.)

Ah, the consolations that offer themselves in age! Death, even – it means not being ill, which means being well. Mind you – Montaigne is always minding us – if you could root out knowledge of pain, you would at the same time eradicate knowledge of pleasure. 'For man, ill can be good in its turn.' Which is also consoling, I suppose, if less persuasively. One seems to have heard something like it propounded in various unsavoury connections.

Death is undoubtedly the most noteworthy action of a person's life. But don't kid yourself that the whole universe is taking note, or that the gods above are working themselves up over it.

Some deaths are more notable than others. Pomponius Atticus, friend of Cicero, was ill, and all attempts to cure him only increased his suffering. He decided to die by starving himself. This course had the effect of restoring him to health. His friends were jubilant, and proposed a celebratory feast, but he told them that since he was bound to die sooner or later, and had gone some way towards dying, he would rather not have to start all over again.

If you have profited from life, then go away satisfied. If life is giving you nothing, why do you still desire it? Montaigne himself wants death to find him planting his cabbages, and not too bothered about leaving the gardening unfinished.

Went for a CT scan (computerized tomography). You recline on a couch and are gently propelled through what resembles a giant washing-machine. I remembered giving something towards its purchase. 'This must be roughly four years old,' I remarked, making to pat the scanner familiarly on its gleaming flank. 'Oh no,' said one of the team, 'this is new: you're thinking of the old magnetic one. It's still around somewhere.' The scanner began to hum complacently.

I made a mental note, hoping the apparatus would pick it up, to exonerate certain types of *useful* computer from the general contumely.

Peter Scupham tells me that once he dreamt he was reading his own obituary under the headline 'Local Man Goes to Heaven'. But the headline was as far as he got. Dreams have a habit of leading us on only to thwart us. On occasion, though, to spare us.

Since, among other things, Scupham is a dealer in second-hand books, it is not too surprising that in another dream he found himself reading a book entitled *A Duck for St George, or Crusading in the Holy Land with Quack and Bill*. A rare item, no doubt, in a once favoured genre. I don't imagine Scupham had time to get much beyond the title.

*

> Dreams, they say, tell stories
> To explain away our woes,
> And so we go on living.

Even nightmares can show mercy. At times, so desperate are a dream's efforts to palliate that the results are ludicrous to the waking mind. Writing of his sufferings from 'the stone', Montaigne adduced the dreamer in Cicero's *De Divinatione* who dreamt he was embracing a girl and found that he had ejaculated his gallstone in the bedclothes. Montaigne wished he had that faculty, but alas his own gallstones had quite put him off girls.

A recurrent explanation by teenagers of why they became pregnant has it that 'There was nothing to do', in which their mothers concur: 'Nothing for them to do around here, is there?' Except watch television – and 'The government should do something,' says one teenager's mother, 'there's too much sex on television.' In my teenage we didn't have all that much to do – school work (reluctantly), reading library books, temperate friendships (same-sex), bike-rides into the countryside (which still existed then, and not far away), a kick around the Rec – but we did it. Also, indoors, spinning yards of cork-wool (what? The word isn't in modern dictionaries), making papier-mâché bowls, shaping round trays with scalloped rims from old gramophone records softened in the oven ... Utterly useless objects, art for art's sake and keeping the kids occupied: all this cost nothing, and no one got pregnant.

The idea of sex as something to do when there was nothing to do would have baffled us, even when we had absolutely nothing to do, or only boring or tiring things. It was something (rather intimidating) to be done when we had grown a good deal cleverer. Or were married, whichever came first. Not that the past was conspicuously better than the present – far from it – but I suspect that in a few important respects it was easier on the young. The young tended to be young then.

Towards the end of 1998 a clinic opened at a Boots store in Glasgow for the purpose of providing condoms for children as young as thirteen. Parents were not to be consulted. Can you believe it? Surely the children would prefer the traditional sort of balloon that has a funny face and goes pop. No more was heard of the clinic, so we may assume it failed in its aim to combat teenage pregnancies and the spread of sexual diseases.

Four years later, as part of a campaign to reduce teenage pregnancies, the Government suggests that parents should leave condoms about the house, as if hidden but not hard to spot, for their children to discover. The idea is that what the kids nick – forbidden fruit as it were – carries more weight than what is urged on them. A possible drawback comes to mind: enterprising youngsters may be led to seek out other buried treasures, such as diamond rings, pearl necklaces, gold watches and credit cards.

When the natives of Tierra del Fuego swarmed round ships from Europe chanting 'yammerschooner', it was assumed they were demanding gifts. It now appears that the expression meant 'be kind to us'. Heartbreaking.

In age, the lurking suspicion that one never knew very much seems to be confirmed. One got by, yes – by a kind of confidence trick, by mimicking, trotting out a limited number of words and set phrases, beginnings that promised to go far but faded out discreetly. All the time one sensed there was a richer language somewhere, and a treasury of experience and knowledge. Like the language of the Maipure people, who lived around the Orinoco River until they were wiped out by a rival tribe towards the end of the eighteenth century, and their language was lost. Except that, even today, a few broken phrases survive in the speech of parrots, erstwhile pets of the Maipure people.

Putting head in gas oven, worried over husband spending too much of his meagre wage on drink, or children refusing what food there was, the rent money, the gas bill (a little extra on the next, but can't be helped). A generation or two later, much has changed. Sick jokes about distracted women sticking heads in electric ovens. Gas ovens had got a bad name. Once there were pink pills for pale people (a bit of a joke), Parrish's Food, cascara sagrada (religiously taken), Sloane's liniment, and the dreaded, unpronounceable, two-way Ipecacuanha Wine – and not much else in the medicine chest in the bathroom. (There may not have been a medicine chest; there may not have been a bathroom.) Nowadays there's a pharmacopoeia in every household, conveniently washed down with a favourite drink. Or of course cars and their assiduous exhausts in the privacy of one's garage. Whatever the means, fluctuating between classes, sexes and ages, suicide is a clumsy experiment, as Schopenhauer noted, whose outcome must remain unknown to the experimenter.

Oh yes, Sylvia Plath resorted to a gas oven as late as 1963. A reviewer of *The Oxford Book of Contemporary Verse* (1980), in which Sylvia Plath was not represented, rebuked the compiler for being unable to come to terms with her. I suppose I had no desire to come to terms with her, and saw no moral, literary, psychiatric or otherwise legitimate obligation to do so. (And what does 'come to terms with' *mean*? Reconcile oneself to? – I would not insult her sad shade by imagining any such presumptuous thing.)

A (relatively) respected newspaper has just printed articles on Sylvia Plath and Marilyn Monroe side by side: established icons, authenticated devotional images, the one highbrow, the other low-neckline. That once celebrated and potent chronicle of sorrows and sickness, *Werther* and its 'vielbeweinter Schatten', was as nothing compared with the ghastly, luxuriant saga of Plath/Hughes.

Selfishly, one has other things to come to terms with, things that are more pressing even though they do not involve poetry or entail a gas oven. And in this one isn't really all that alone. The world isn't populated solely by prurient or self-seeking readers and writers avid for copy. It only seems that way.

An Indian scholar working on 'Sylvia Plath as a Modernist' e-mails a British university to seek guidance on enrolling for a D.Litt.: 'Modernism has been my keen interest and I have investigated the problems been faced by the poets who led troubled lives. Their obsession with death, their encounter with death tragically and the confessions recorded in their immortal works, has prompted me to still go deep down and probe extensively and intensively in to their lives and works.' Sounds somewhat like a cystoscopy. Literature needs its physicians.

Like other people, poets led troubled lives, confessed, and encountered death long before modernism, motors and medications came along. But 'contemporary', as Erich Heller remarked, is a 'queer term of praise with which some critics appear to have replaced the older virtue of timelessness'.

In Vernon Scannell's new novel, *Feminine Endings*, about a creative-writing centre up north, a businessman explains his presence: 'As you can imagine, I don't get much time for reading. That's partly why I thought poetry would be a good thing to get into. I mean because it's shorter and it's got what you might call cachet.'

Cachet? So that's it! How remote from my young days, when poetry – the reading of it, let alone the creatively writing of it – got you a bad name, or a mixture of bad names.

'Cachet' also signifies (I quote *The Concise Oxford Dictionary*) 'a flat capsule enclosing a dose of unpleasant-tasting medicine'. That's more like it.

'No one could tell from these translations that Goethe was a great poet': the complaint has often been heard. Bedevilled by considerations of contemporariness and timelessness, such translations are indisputably dispiriting. There is no better translator of Goethe into English today than David Luke, and yet ... The unwieldy abstractions roll out like banks of storm clouds, portentous and platitudinous, frequently in binary blasts: 'Freud und Schmerz', 'Geist und Körper', 'Luft und Lüftchen', 'ewige Gefühle', 'ewig Schöne', 'Weltseele', 'O Allumklammernde', 'Des hohen Himmels fruchtende Fülle', 'Lieb und Leben', 'O Erd, o Sommer!', O Glück, o Lust' ... Luke has no choice but to follow. Could you tell there was a great poet here? If not, can you honestly blame the translator? (Small chance of his living up to Goethe's saying, that translators are pimps busily cracking up the charms of some half-veiled beauty, and exciting an irresistible desire for the original.)

Interestingly it is the finest of the perfect, simple-seeming lyrics, long held the least translatable, that come out best in English. However, Luke outlines a problem: Goethe's poetry is 'of the essence of German' and, unfortunately for the translator, 'the converse is also true: the poetry of the German language is of the essence of Goethe'. The idea strikes me as interesting, not to say arcane, but not quite real. Hölderlin is eminently translatable, so is a fair amount of Heine, the same (or more) is true of Rilke (possibly his idiosyncratic way with words emboldens the translator), and as for Brecht, you can hardly go wrong with him. In any case, even if Goethe is seen as inarguably *sui generis*, Luke's practice belies his theory.

There is an alternative Goethe, as Dionysian, subversive and mischievous as elsewhere he is Apollonian, authoritarian and earnest: the author of the *Roman Elegies* and *The Diary* (both translated splendidly by David Luke, the latter and parts of the former made public relatively lately), epigrams (some long suppressed), passages from *Faust* (often featuring Mephistopheles, 'the spirit who always denies'), the novel *Elective Affinities* (scandalous and irreproachable), and impromptu pronouncements and asides recorded by Eckermann and others close to him. Whatever those 'essences', Goethe was not subject to them. This emperor is flesh and blood, unbuttoned; at times he hardly seems to be wearing any clothes at all.

In *Trains of Thought* Victor Brombert writes about the English classes in a Paris lycée during the 1930s:

> Our most memorable *prof d'anglais*, Monsieur Labé, appeared to me as uncanny as Coleridge's ancient mariner, whom he seemed determined to reincarnate. He too had a long grey beard and a glittering eye . . . With a visionary look, Monsieur Labé would raise himself full height from his desk chair, book in hand, one arm outstretched, and declaim the opening lines in solemn fashion. He became a seer, and no longer saw us. Yet he was not ridiculous. His vatic manner amused but also impressed us. I was titillated by the sound effects of his nasal chant and the marked scanning.
>
> > The fair breeze blew, the white foam flew,
> > The furrow followed free . . .
>
> It was then and there, and not in my French classes, that I first tasted the delights of alliteration and assonance.
>
> Monsieur Labé could become quite oracular, and then his forked beard would respond by flowing in separate directions, as though agitated by the conflictual winds of inspiration. He initiated us to Wordsworth's sonnet:

> The world is too much with us; late and soon,
> Getting and spending, we lay waste our powers:
> Little we see in Nature that is ours;
> We have given our hearts away, a sordid boon!

I did not quite understand what a 'sordid boon' could possibly be, nor why it deserved an exclamation mark. Nor did I have a clear idea of how and to whom we had given our hearts away. The words 'spending' and 'powers' also remained somewhat foggy in the context. But no matter. Something did click.

Every school should have a Monsieur Labé. (I reproduce him here by kind permission of W. W. Norton & Company.)

'A lazar-house it seemed.' Ghastly spasm, or racking torture, convulsions, epilepsies, fierce catarrhs, intestine stone and ulcer, colic pangs, pining atrophy, marasmus, dropsies, asthmas, and joint-racking rheums ... All ascribed to 'th'inabstinence' of Eve, whose daughters are much in demand as nurses.

'Nor love thy life, nor hate; but what thou livest, live well.' Excellent advice, Michael. Unfortunately we're not all of us archangels.

Scholars say that Milton depicts Eve's dreaming as irresponsible fancy ('fantasy'), and Adam's as showing a more discerning imagination. (Along the lines of Coleridge's distinction.) But is this the case? Would Adam or Eve have dreamt at all, prelapsarianly? Wouldn't their sleep be tranquil, untroubled, like (as we hopefully put it) a baby's? It was after the Fall that we came to need dreams as solace, or deserve them as penance. They can hark back briefly to a state of innocence; they can point up the anxieties, sorrows, crimes and terrors of our waking life.

But 'our two first parents' did dream, it seems. Normally, we gather, Eve dreamt of Adam or of work done or to be done. (At that time work and pleasure were one and the same; eating bread in the sweat of one's face came later.) Her famous 'dream' – when Satan, squatting like a toad close at her ear, assayed 'by his devilish art to reach/ The organs of her fancy', and raise 'at least distempered, discontented thoughts,/ Vain hopes, vain aims, inordinate desires', until disturbed by Ithuriel with his angelic spear – was no dream generated within, but involuntary hypnopaedia, 'fraudulent temptation', seduction from without.

When comforting Eve (who had gone some way to comforting herself: 'how glad I waked/ To find this but a dream!'), Adam showed himself so knowledgeable on the subject – the fault lies not with fancy, whose important role is to serve reason by forming shapes from information passed on by the five senses, but with 'mimic fancy', which takes over when true fancy sleeps and, 'misjoining shapes,/ Wild work produces oft, and most in dreams' – that we wonder what he customarily dreamt of. In the absence of evidence, we may suppose, of God, or work done or to be done, and of Eve. His only recorded 'dream', of witnessing in detail the creation of his helpmate, occurred 'as in a trance', or as if partly anaesthetized (the least one would expect while having a rib removed). No discerning imagination at work there.

Eve's other noteworthy dream comes near the end of the poem, while Michael is apprising Adam (man to man) of what the future holds. A sweet dream, too, free from irresponsible fancy, discontented thoughts or inordinate desires. 'For God is also in sleep,' she tells Adam, 'and dreams advise,/ Which he hath sent propitious, some great good/ Presaging': that, despite her 'wilful crime', 'by me the Promised Seed shall all restore.' God has spoken to her, in gentle tones, by way of the Archangel Michael, giver of dreams. This is one of the very finest passages in Milton.

'The only two of mankind, but in them/ The whole included race.' The notion of Eve as a passive *tertium quid*, an uncomprehending bystander at the feast of intellect, won't do. Compared with her – though not in her fond eyes – Adam is something of a dull (but faithful) dog. Earlier, when Raphael and Adam discourse on astronomy, Eve wanders off to tend her fruits and flowers: not because she wouldn't have understood – Milton is perfectly clear on the point – but because she preferred to hear about it from her spouse, who would 'intermix grateful digressions' and 'conjugal caresses': 'from his lip/ Not words alone pleased her'. She was learning how to make the best of both worlds.

Talking along these lines to first-year students in Singapore, I was taken to task by a severe-looking Chinese nun of mature years: 'But all this is only Milton!' I mildly deplored the word 'only' and mumbled something about God moving in a mysterious way. Clearly the nun couldn't see God ever moving in *that* mysterious a way. She dropped English the following year.

Sister D., the Irish head of the English department of the Convent of the Holy Infant Jesus, a highly respected school in Singapore, would have had no great problem with Milton. She was known to be of the opinion that Antony and Cleopatra would be received into heaven since, although not married, they were truly in love with each other. Shakespeare's Antony and Cleopatra, that would be.

'Not only does the Darwinian theory command superabundant power to explain. Its economy in doing so has a sinewy elegance, a poetic beauty that outclasses even the most haunting of the world's origin myths': thus Richard Dawkins writing in *River Out of Eden* (a Miltonic echo) with an elegance of his own. 'There is more poetry in Mitochondrial Eve than in her mythological namesake.' ('Mito-chondrion: a small spherical or rodlike body, bounded by a double membrane, in the cytoplasm of most cells: contains enzymes responsible for energy production,' says *Collins English Dictionary*.) A busy little body, this Darwinian Eve! Small, spherical or rodlike –

but there's no accounting for tastes. Milton, you should be living at this hour! But you are, and so is your Eve.

A small Singapore publisher by the name of Cultured Lotus has proposed to reprint my *Memoirs of a Mendicant Professor* (1969) for the local, Malaysian and Hong Kong market. A week later Cultured Lotus backs out. While there is no 'theoretical' problem with the Singapore Ministry of Information and the Arts, the publisher fears they wouldn't find a printer for the book or a distributor or bookstores bold enough to stock it. Cultured Lotus, he says, would like to go on leading a quiet life, unknown and anonymous.

How ridiculous, one might think, thirty-one years after the book's publication in London and its discreet banning in Singapore, and forty years after my initial brush with Lee Kuan Yew's ruling party. (Over something to do with culture.) But this is the nicest way of preserving an orderly, compliant, industrious and highly prosperous little country: a mild, bearable, ever-present fearfulness. Happy the land that doesn't feel a need for heroes.

Our Prime Minister is attacked for philistinism and anti-elitism, notably by Sir Vidia Naipaul and Doris Lessing. But a democratic government is supposed to serve the majority of the electorate, not some elite, and hence a Ministry of Culture, Media and Sport busies itself largely with the more popular of these tricky charges. A prime minister who quoted *Hamlet* in his speeches would require the remedial services of an exceptionally gifted spin-doctor, whereas an occasional carefully chosen allusion to *EastEnders* will go down a treat at the pub. If it's the nation that's imposing what Naipaul terms 'an aggressively plebeian culture' on Mr Blair, Mr Blair isn't putting up much resistance. For all I know, he may read Anita Brookner and listen to Anton Bruckner in the privacy of his bedroom, but somehow I doubt it. He is a man of his time, the past is of little consequence, his time is him. His duties are heavy, his recreations light. It is the company of friends that he prizes, the like-minded, not of captious literati.

And can you blame people for 'philistinism', when a farm animal pickled in formaldehyde is the inescapable wonder of the galleries, an 'artist's' unmade bed fetches £150,000, and the director of a 'brutal sex shocker' proclaims that the theatre must be 'not timid, not comfortable, . . . It is like a bullfight.' The great enemy of art is bad art. Where are the enemies of bad art, and what are they doing? Keeping their heads down? It's true that their grumblings don't make good or durable copy; they soon take on the aspect of spoilsports and holier-than-thous – the bugaboos of the media and of media-led democracy. As for elitism, with young Leverkühn in mind, one might ask oneself whether epochs that possessed such a thing knew the word at all, or used it.

Writers are free to criticize, complain and contest; they can't expect governments to reward them for doing so. And patronage is never far from patronizing. Yet in fact there are valuable prizes around, and lots of grants. The odd knighthood or dameship is dished out, and a generous scattering of CBEs and OBEs, for unspecified 'services to literature', and even, among humbler oldies whose offences are forgotten or were never noticed, civil list pensions. No one is sent to prison or exiled.

British writers have long been exceptionally fortunate. So why this unseemly longing to be loved and treasured by the secular powers?

> Under a Sovereign
> who despised culture
> Arts and Letters improved –

Auden doesn't say whether the artists and men of letters themselves enjoyed any improvement in their creature comforts, but they were not positively hindered in their creative labours.

'Of comfort no man speak'; 'These elegies are to this generation in no way consolatory'; 'I tell you naught for your comfort'. How low they have fallen, these once noble rejections of spurious comfort and consolation. These days they proudly preface some routine discharge of studied nastiness or squalor. Mostly coming from the word processors of individuals who have never fallen foul of the authorities, who have led pretty comfortable lives.

You might have thought it was irony, in line with Swift's *Modest Proposal* . . .

A 'quality' Sunday paper runs an article headed 'A good reason to stop being hypocritical about porn', on the popularity and commercial success of 'the international adult entertainment industry', the only business on the Internet consistently turning a profit. Yet we British are 'frozen in a kind of moral Dark Ages': nearly all the pornography we buy 'by the bucketload' is generated abroad. Our money flows only one way – out. In the US and elsewhere in Europe profitability runs as high as 2,000 per cent; there are said to be some 200,000 active sex sites accessible from one's home PC. Only when our laws are reformed can we develop legitimate taxpaying, global businesses and compete in this flourishing market.

The writer detests hypocrisy; the insinuation that it is a tribute vice pays to virtue is a frivolous French joke: neither virtue nor vice plays any part here, or only figuratively as commercial success or commercial failure. He doesn't drag in the tired old contention common in the arms trade that if we don't oblige dubious regimes someone else will ('Pray tell me why we may not also go smacks?'). There's no irony here, that puerile artifice, ignorance posing as simulated ignorance. Just one simple all-subjugating idea: the 'good reason'.

How assiduously the intelligentsia shepherd us down the primrose path!

'Among the many agents of the public's spiritual debilitation, it is

the voyeuristic genre of biography that takes the cake. That there
are far more ruined maidens than immortal lyrics seems to give
pause to nobody. The last bastion of realism, biography is based on
the breathtaking premise that art can be explained by life': Joseph
Brodsky.

'In the end, the gift of writing novels is not unlike God's grace: it
is arbitrary, incomprehensible and sublimely unjust. It is not a
scandal if novelists of genius prove to be wretched fellows; it is a
comforting miracle that wretched fellows prove to be novelists of
genius': Simon Leys.

Well, yes, one responds guardedly to both statements, which may
seem to edge a little too close to the theory that normal standards of
behaviour don't apply to 'immortal poets' or 'novelists of genius', a
theory most commonly promoted by charlatans. Which these two
men are not.

I know nothing of Joseph Brodsky personally; only some of his
writings, which tell one a lot about him as a writer (which is enough
for me). Going by what little I know of him personally, Simon Leys
(i.e. Pierre Ryckmans) is a good person. He is for certain a sweet-
natured writer, except when faced with the likes of Mao Zedong.
Still, if someone comes up with a biography of him, I shall hasten
not to read it.

'It is not that one doesn't want to know about Simone de Beauvoir's
trademark turban, or Jane Gallop's penchant for sex with 36-year-
old men, or whether Mary McCarthy shaved her legs (she didn't)':
London Review of Books. One had better want to know if one wants to
keep one's good name.

Dear dead artist! All those years of striving, of sacrifice, of self-doubt,
of manifest failure and obscure success. A life of hard graft at your
desk – and what for? That someone should write a book about your
life in bed.

*

Those experts on the lives, somatic and psycho, of other people! One of them asserts that Rupert Brooke's semen sometimes came out green. Another says it was his urine. If they can't agree on so colourful a point, how can we trust them to get anything right?

David Ellis, author of the third volume of the Cambridge biography of D. H. Lawrence, has observed: 'Trying to prevent a posthumous invasion of all one's private doings, when the only real protection is a life wholly dull and uninteresting, is like putting a finger in the dike. Sooner or later the insatiable public appetite for gossip bursts through.' Even that 'real protection' isn't inevitably reliable: just think of the seductive challenge posed by a clean slate, a blank page.

A resident of Hull informs me that his local branch of W. H. Smith has created a new subject section called 'Biography/True Crime'.

Our highbrow police ... In a Manchester suburb a bookmaker's was being burgled. The police were alerted, but although they had a station nearby they took two hours to get to the scene. They said they had been looking for a place that made books.

'Great legs', 'slim build', 'sexy voice', 'penetrating green eyes', 'of abundant voltage', 'passionate', 'French background' ... But also 'doctoral-degreed': the personals in the *New York Review of Books*, as you might expect, revel in books (alternatively, the 'written word', 'poetry', 'reading'). 'SINGLE BOOKLOVERS gets unattached people acquainted.' Books do furnish a bedroom.

A group of fifteen young authors, calling themselves the New Puritans, have come up with ten rules. In the arts, rules are made to be broken: a reason why one shouldn't turn up one's nose at them. Rules you can actually articulate – without drowning in an ocean of provisos – won't amount to much, but may be of interest as indicating aspiration and abjuration.

'1. Primarily story-tellers, we are dedicated to the narrative form.' (Fair enough, a story-teller should tell a story.)

'2. We are prose writers and recognize that it is the dominant form of expression. For this reason we shun poetry and poetic licence in all its forms.' (Their privilege. Prose writers usually do well to avoid poetic prose. The juxtaposition of 'shun' and 'in all its forms' brings out the secondary definitions of 'licence': 'disregard of law or propriety, abuse of freedom' and 'licentiousness'. The true voice of the puritan in one of the word's meanings: someone practising or affecting extreme strictness in religion or morals. Nowadays, and despite all the licence at hand, poetry has little truck with religion or morals, but think of Horace; 'Poets aim either to benefit, or to amuse, or to utter words at once both pleasing and helpful to life.' Delete 'to amuse' and this might even smack of morals.)

'3. While acknowledging the value of genre fiction, whether classical or modern, we will always move towards new openings, rupturing existing genre expectations.' (Unexceptionable and expected – note the exciting, if somewhat surgical, violence of 'rupturing' – although the term 'genre' is imprecise and top-heavy outside such clear-cut applications as science fiction and bodice ripper. New openings betoken or promise new genres. Can anything be genreless? If so, genrelessness is a genre.)

'4. We believe in textual simplicity and vow to avoid all devices of voice, rhetoric, authorial asides.' (Simplicity is a lovely thing, but not always altogether possible. Note the religious – or is it rhetorical? – connotations of 'vow'. Because thou art virtuous, shall there be no more cakes and ale?, no more voice or asides? Tell us what *will* there be.)

'5. In the name of clarity, we recognize the importance of temporal linearity and eschew flashbacks, dual temporal narrative and foreshadowing.' (Aristotle, I think, said something about aiming for as much clarity as the subject allows. 'Only in limitation is mastery shown,' decreed Goethe, a man of illimitable interests and powers. You never know when a flashback will come in handy, or a touch of foreshadowing, but you have to be rather clever to get away with these devices.)

'6. We believe in grammatical purity and avoid any elaborate punctuation.' (We all believe in purity, don't we? As for punctuation, it depends on how elaborate 'elaborate' is; an example would help.)

'7. We recognize that published works are also historical documents. As fragments of time, all our texts are dated and set in the present day. All products, places, artists and objects named are real.' (The majority of published works don't last long enough to become historical in any respect or sense. 'Set in the present day' would have eliminated much of Dickens, Thackeray, Tolstoy, Balzac, Thomas Mann, and other great story-tellers. This rule sounds like publicity for organic food. Or like a recipe for libel.)

'8. As faithful representations of the present, our texts will avoid all improbable or unknowable speculation about the past or the future.' (Are the New Puritans restricting themselves to vignettes and *faits divers*? Or are they purely determined to live up to their self-designation, that old word 'puritan'?)

'9. We are moralists, so all texts feature a recognizable ethical reality.' (Fine, were it not that we distrust people who announce themselves as moralists. Some of us don't care for that jargonic 'text', but possibly the New Puritans are thinking of the word's medieval sense of 'Gospel', and its modern usage: a passage drawn from Scripture as the subject of a sermon.)

'10. Nevertheless, our aim is integrity of expression, above and beyond any commitment to form.' (At last a nevertheless. A good note to end on: no one can quarrel with integrity, whatever the rest of the sentence may mean.)

It's too easy to make fun of rules, other people's. In an engaging article in *The Times*, Nicholas Blincoe, one of the New Puritans, says of this 'once in a generation call to arms': 'If New Puritanism is anything, it is an attempt to embrace what we do where we do it and who we do it with.' (Perhaps not a hundred per cent pure grammatically, but all their texts are set in the present day, whereas 'whom' is stuck fast in the past.) Also, almost disarmingly: 'It seems possible that we have genuinely found the holy rules of literature (or maybe eighty per cent of them; the problem is that none of us can agree on which eight out of the ten are the essential ones).'

Good luck to the fearless fifteen. My guess is they'll survive their rules. Goethe declared that 'The novel is a subjective epic in which the author requests permission to treat the world in his own way. So the only question is whether he has a way.'

Rebelliousness, whether the enemy be repression or indulgence, is what gives the young writer lift-off. Even the blasé look on with wonder. Then the rocket boosters fall away, and with seeming sedateness the craft moves on into deeper space. But no one wants to know.

'We shun poetry.' That delight in tropes and images: the lady's feet were 'three-inch golden lilies, graced by tiny shoes made like the mountain-crow, with tips embroidered to look like the claws', and she moved 'like a tender young willow shoot in a spring breeze', or with 'the graceful gliding flight of a swallow'. The custom of foot-binding is attributed to the Chinese poet Li Yü or Li Houzhu (936/7–78), third and last emperor of the Southern Tang Dynasty, who conceived the poetical idea of enabling his favourite concubine to dance on the likeness of a lotus flower. It took a revolution, early twentieth century, to silence this poetry.

Poeticisms in another sphere bring home how pathetically

impoverished the West is in its erotic vocabulary. For example, 'the butterfly flutters about, searching for flowery scents', 'the queen bee making honey', 'the hungry steed gallops to the feed crib', 'striking the silver swan with a golden ball', 'making candles by dipping the wick in tallow' and 'fetching fire behind the hill'. The innocent young bride in the seventeenth-century novel, *The Prayer Mat of Flesh* (anglicized as *The Before Midnight Scholar*), rejects this exercise because turning one's back on one's husband is an offence against decorum.

These are a few of the thirty-six practices of 'vernal dalliance' celebrated by the poets of the Tang period. Aside from a limited stock of dysphemisms, all we can boast of is the dispiriting 'missionary position'.

I am reminded of a poignant comment by a Thai student of mine: 'Poetry makes the world, the nature, have more technique colour than it really was.'

Two new books bear titles that the New Puritans won't be alone in deprecating: *Taking Off Emily Dickinson's Clothes* and *Sleeping with Jane Austen*. The former is poetry, less than Donnean, concerning the complexity of women's undergarments in nineteenth-century America; the latter is a novel whose protagonist keeps one of Jane Austen's books under his pillow to save it from being nicked.

In a poem about the London suburb in which I live, these lines occur: 'If I told my neighbours, We must love one another or – ,/ I would die of shame. Or else they would kill me.' Am tickled to find the implied quote in Robert Conquest's list of resounding pronouncements which don't sound so fine once you pause to think. 'Among the century's most quoted lines/ Are some that don't send shivers up our spines.' For instance:

> Clearly the writer forgot
> In the end we must all of us die if we love one another or not.
> To do Auden justice, when he next went through it
> He gave it a questioning look, and then he withdrew it.

Conquest's other impostors are 'April is the cruellest month' (Eliot), 'The Lord survives the rainbow of His will' (Lowell), 'Do not go gentle into that good night' (Dylan Thomas), and 'A terrible beauty is born' (Yeats).

'Homo sum; humani nil a me alienum puto' (Terence): another of those noble declarations that bring a nice warm glow to the heart. But then – unless 'human' is to be set sharply apart from 'inhuman', in which case the claim has little meaning – it may strike us that there are quite a number of human things which are alien to quite a number of us. Including the killing of babies. Dear me, Blake!: 'Sooner murder an infant in its cradle than nurse unacted desires.' Today that would get you put away, not without reason.

'So far as we are human, what we do must be either evil or good; so far as we do evil or good, we are human; and it is better, in a paradoxical way, to do evil than to do nothing; at least we exist.' Eliot's manner here, in his essay on Baudelaire, is urbane and knowing, impellingly logical. It instils in us the agreeable feeling that we are perfectly at home in elevated circles. The matter, once you grasp it, is pretty dreadful, comforting in its creepy way ('sooner murder an infant . . .'). Some assumption, some paradox!

The essay is dated 1930, when Eliot was forty-two years old, and at least no death camps were in unquestionable evidence. And after his account of the miserable state of affairs he sees around him, the world of electoral reform, sex reform and dress reform (a motley assemblage of ogres), no doubt the theoretical possibility of damnation came as some sort of relief, as 'an immediate form of salvation from the ennui of modern life'. As a sixth former I chose the *Selected Essays* for a school prize, and was much taken with Eliot's analogy between the cheery modern idea of 'sexual operation' and Kruschen Salts, a popular fizzy pick-me-up I was partial to.

Coat-trailing? Some coat, some trail! The passage is reminiscent of Rupert Brooke, finding peace a frightful bore and thanking God for furnishing a war and a timely opportunity to turn away, 'as swimmers into cleanness leaping', from 'a world grown old and cold and weary'. Both Brooke's rhetoric and Eliot's are self-regarding: the fate of other people counts for little beside the condition of the speaker's soul.

'It is this, I believe, that Baudelaire is trying to express': so Eliot is merely helping the Frenchman out? The most striking moment in *Journaux Intimes*, an English version of which Eliot was reviewing, runs thus: 'True civilization doesn't lie in gas, or in steam, or in table-turning. It lies in the diminution of the traces of original sin.' The tendency of Baudelaire's thought is clear, says Eliot, though 'it is not quite clear exactly what *diminution* here implies'.

By the nature of original sin, its diminution must seem an impossible happening. And equally, we suppose, any diminution of its traces, its workings in our life. And we might suspect that Eliot wouldn't consider the phenomenon especially desirable. Yet with God all things are possible. And the idea that true civilization would or could consist not in material inventions or spiritualist superstition or religiosity but in some reduction in the burden of sin, of innate depravity, we all carry and suffer from – that idea is at least a decent one. Baudelaire could be insufferable, but he wasn't sanctimonious; there was no soul-snobbery about him.

(A puzzle here, maybe, for that mysterious academic discipline known as Practical Theology to work on.)

It has been said that the full rehabilitation of the Marquis de Sade began only after 1945, 'with the discovery of the evil which humans are capable of organizing'. This, I take it, means that in comparison with the agents of the Holocaust the Marquis was indeed practically divine.

In a piece in the *London Review of Books* Richard Davenport-Hines mentions some of the tricks Sade got up to. In Paris in 1763 he was charged with blasphemy and sodomy after offering money to a fan-maker and requesting her to whip him while he masturbated with the aid of a crucifix. In 1768, during Easter as it happened, he subjected an indignant middle-aged working woman to an ordeal of flagellation. In 1772 he fell foul of a Marseille brothel-keeper and was accused of sodomy and of poisoning two prostitutes by administering candies soaked in Spanish fly. After eloping with his wife's younger sister in 1777 and organizing a more than usually ambitious orgy at his château, he was arrested under a *lettre de cachet* issued by Louis XVI. 'His calvary of thirteen years' incarceration began.'

His *what?*

We perceive that the Holocaust as a yardstick of acceptability, serving to absolve or mitigate lesser evils, hasn't let Mother Teresa, Florence Nightingale or Father Damien off the hook, or even your mum and dad. In any case, they are insufficiently exciting to warrant or indeed afford a 'full rehabilitation'. A book denouncing or exposing Florence Nightingale is to say the least publishable. Not so a book defending her.

A couple have had to move church because the Vicar of Cheadle would not tolerate the singing of 'Jerusalem' at their marriage ceremony. The objections to this hymn or song or poem (words by William Blake) were (a) it was nationalistic, invoking 'England' three times; (b) it failed to praise God: a reference to 'the Countenance Divine' cut no ice (the Marquis was divine); and (c) it had nothing to say about love or marriage: a mention of 'arrows of desire' was best left unexamined.

Further objections might include the Holy Lamb of God as seen on our pleasant pastures: atrociously bad taste at a time of foot-and-mouth; the misplaced sneer at heavy industry: 'dark Satanic mills'; incitement to violence: 'Nor shall my sword sleep in my hand'; and above all the speaker's crazy resolve to establish Jerusalem in some English green-belt area – as if we didn't have trouble enough already, what with the IRA, asylum seekers, fulminating imams and multiculturalism.

But the Vicar recognizes the gravest objection: 'What the words are actually saying is, "Wouldn't it be nice if Jesus lived in England?"' Not in his backyard; it wouldn't be nice at all: for one thing, a lot of clerics could lose their jobs.

Look! Is it Superman? Is it Batman? Is it Spiderman? No, it's Jesusman!

How good the Church is at driving the faithful away.

Churchgoers are being urged to deposit cards carrying the image of a cross and the words 'What would love do now?' inside telephone boxes. The cards, described as 'prostitute-style' and 'pimp-sized', are produced by the Churches' Advertising Network in preparation for the Christmas season. No phone number is offered, no vital statistics are revealed, no intimation is given of what love might do, and (thanks be to God) the campaign makes no mention of Jesus.

A clergyman, formerly an advertising executive, explains: 'The problem with the way churches communicate has been this reliance on traditional imagery.' Call-girl communications pasted in phone boxes are not traditional if only because phone boxes are not quite traditional yet. (Of the status of call-girls one is not wholly sure.) As for Jesus, if you wish to spare your weak stomach, maybe you can take him out of Christianity, but watch your nomenclature: take Christ out and what you are left with sounds much like inanity.

(This news item appeared in the issue of *The Times* dated 12 September 2001 and mainly devoted to the terrorist attacks on New

York and Washington of the previous day. Which made it look all the sillier – but at least agreeably unalarming in marking the limits of the Anglican Church's daring, dedication and desperation.)

Again, that vocabulary of religion which one might have supposed lost to sight and hearing ... President Bush's talk of a 'crusade against terrorism' would provoke hardly a glimmer of recognition (let alone a twinge of unease) in the West, where 'crusade' is current only in the secondary sense, 'a vigorous campaign in favour of a cause', but has angered Muslim commentators, who have longer religious memories and detect in this 'Freudian slip' a desire in the West to resume those ancient wars against Islam.

The Bush Administration's high-flown battle-cry, 'Operation Infinite Justice' made matters worse, since infinite justice is something only Allah can administer. (Odd that this consideration hadn't occurred, *mutatis mutandis*, to Christians.) 'Operation Infinite Justice' was later downgraded, losing much of its divine flavour, to 'Operation Enduring Freedom'.

As the poet wrote in one of his more pensive moods: 'In life we barely choose our words even,/ Only those we hurt will still recall them.'

Poetry is generally the second or third casualty when war draws close.

> We will not waver,
> We will not tire,
> We will not falter,
> And we will not fail.
> Peace and freedom will prevail.
> – George W. Bush

As the last lights flicker out and the hubbub sinks into silence, a recorded mantra patters on unheard, mankind's elegy or eulogy: 'wwwdotearthdotorgdotends'.

'The smell of a hospital,' Wislawa Szymborska confesses, 'makes me sick.' 'Language, the oldest but still the most reliable guide to a people's true sentiments, starkly reveals the intimate connection between illness and indignity. In English, we use the same word to describe an expired passport, an indefensible argument, an illegitimate legal document, and a person disabled by disease. We call each of them invalid': Thomas Szasz. And then, I suppose, there's the demeaning word 'patient'.

When Dr B. announced, more in anger than in sorrow, that the 'carpet of tumours' he had removed from my innocent bladder was directly caused by smoking, I didn't want to seem ungrateful, and proposed a bargain: if he would go on excising whatever tumours might turn up, I would renounce smoking – after sixty-two years. That was in early June of 2001. And so, rather to my surprise, I did. There were bad moments, but I have not smoked since that day – except in dreams, when to my horror, I find myself puffing happily away while chatting with old friends, and cry out in an access of shame more overpowering than anything in waking life could engender in me. Awake, I have to convince myself that it was only a dream, for which I accept minimal responsibility.

Now Dr B. has transferred to another London hospital. Must I continue to honour the agreement? – which I'm not absolutely sure Dr B. was ever aware of, he being eager at the time to follow the consultant closely round the ward rather than hobnob with exigent patients. Does it matter whether I smoke or not, given my age, etc.? These are insidious considerations: get thee behind me! My friend Petra Lewis, a former smoker, reminds me that the first six months are the worst, and it would be perverse to capitulate now. A more vulgar, more powerful argument against back-sliding is that I'm saving money. Vulgar it may be, but the thought provokes a rare, rosy glow, makes me feel undilutedly virtuous.

Let us have medicos of our own maturity,
For callow practitioners incline to be casual
   with a middle-aged party.

Doctors in their thirties are loath to labour
   over sick men in their sixties.
Such are near their natural end: respect nature.

To save us suffering or them their pains,
   physicians in their fifties
Are prepared to surrender us senior citizens.

Let our medical attendants be of compatible years,
Who will think of us as in certain respects their peers,

Who know what we possibly still have to live for,
Why we are not unfailingly poised to withdraw.

Yet for the giving of enemas or injections,
   let there be youthful nurses
With steady hands, clear heads, and other attractions.

Whether physicians or patients, we all can appreciate
A pretty miss, or (it may be) her male associate.

Then permit us to be appreciative and appreciated
A little, in our final fruition, however belated.

What goes in had better come out, and fairly promptly. A jug measures your productivity, and a nurse keeps a strict account. If output falls, you'll be kept in hospital for another day or two. Getting out of bed, jug in hand, I have a brief dizzy spell and spill a little of the precious fluid. The curtains drawn, I top up the calibrated jug from the water jug. It's not really cheating. In any case, a bleeping scanner, shaped like a mole, will announce the persisting presence of so many millilitres of urine in the bladder. I promise the nurses, to whom the doctors defer on this point, the nurses being closer to the patient, that I'll do better in the privacy of my own loo. Finally – 'if your wife wants you back' – they let me go home.

There's a large poster in the ward detailing in vivid colours the various kinds of urological cancer – kidney, bladder, prostate, testicular – to which men are particularly or solely heir. One takes a quick glance at it on the way to the lavatories. Thank you – it's enough to know about what one knows one has.

To check for testicular cancer one should feel for an untoward lump. Since many of us men are squeamish for some reason, it is suggested that one's partner might (more pleasingly?) take on this little service. Enough to put one right off partners!

In St George's again, for further probing and removing of tissue for biopsy. My neighbour is Eric, old, shrunken, lugubrious, bent double as if about to topple forward, but able to shuffle along at speed, his feet moving like pistons, even though he can't possibly see where he is going. Last night he had a strenuous nightmare and fell out of bed, waking us all up. Nurses and patients alike tease him, just a little. He sees it as a compliment.

Eric has his moments, usually powered by simple indignations. A new, motherly nurse asks him, 'Have you opened your bowels, Eric?' He can't understand the question, or pretends not to. 'Wha'?' She repeats, slowly, clearly: 'Have you opened your bowels today?' 'Opened my bowels?' he says incredulously. 'I can't bloody close them!' We could have told her that.

'Cowards die many times before their deaths; the valiant never taste of death but once.' Sonorous words, but not the whole story. The coward keeps on 'dying' – that is, not quite dying – and tasting the freshness of life regained, feeling a rush of affection for the everyday, or a touch of triumph at walking out of hospital under one's own steam. And this many times perhaps. But for the valiant, afraid of nothing, not even once. Valour, a bit of a bore, even (dare one say) a wet blanket, must be its own reward.

'A man does not know whose hands will stroke from him the last bubbles of his life. That alone should make him kinder to strangers': Richard Selzer.

Voluntary euthanasia had apparently been legalized, under certain strict conditions, and we were taking advantage of it – with what were surely sound and sufficient reasons.

We checked in, as arranged, at an establishment recognized for the purpose and managed by a middle-aged lady of dignified and slightly severe mien. The chamber into which she led us was spacious and elegant, aside from the double futon on the floor, rumpled as if the previous occupants had left in a hurry. It would have been petty, or unwise, to complain. The lady manageress declined to discuss the mode of operation; it was a subject her well-bred clients never broached. Most likely it involved a deadly gas. Just for a moment I felt sick with dread. But there was no going back, no thought of it. We were presented with a tasteless meal, and grew drowsy – the gas beginning to work? – and soon drifted off, hand in hand as the prospectus had suggested.

Before long we were both awake again. A cylindrical gauge on the wall at my back, I noticed, registered a bright red, indicating maximum intensity; the corresponding gauge behind my wife showed nothing. The manageress failed to hide her chagrin. It seemed we would have to be taken to the local post office, a mile or two away, where the facilities, if less comfortable ('no frills'), were more reliable, the deadly gas presumably deadlier. We were loaded into the back of a small van, but on arrival found the post office closed: not surprisingly, it being by now the middle of the night. So back we went to the original establishment, where we were grudgingly given another meal. (I began to worry about the state of my bowels: the idea was to achieve a reasonably dignified exit.)

At some point my wife left the room, and returned in daytime garb. I remained in my pyjamas. The manageress's mood had changed to petulance: somehow the unprecedented fiasco was down to us, specifically to me . . .

There being nowhere further for it to go, the dream stopped. I woke up – it was a little after 2 a.m. – asking myself why there should have been such a discrepancy between the reading on my gauge and that on my wife's (I was tempted to rouse her), wondering bemusedly whether we would get a rebate from the establishment, telling myself there could be no interrogating dreams, and it was, was it not, no more than a dream. At the same time dead tired and wide awake, I had difficulty in getting to sleep again.

'A dream, the other night, that the world had become dissatisfied with the inaccurate manner in which facts are reported, and had employed me, with a salary of a thousand dollars, to report things of public importance exactly as they happen.' A rather fine, civically responsible dream, which Nathaniel Hawthorne must have found gratifying, but others are likely to consider less than thrilling.

It's no wonder that people flinch away when you set out to tell them your dreams. All those powerful emotions lacking (to use Eliot's coinage) any 'objective correlative', without a factual context, situation or chain of events which would account for, bring alive, and define those emotions – and thus enable the teller to convey them authentically to the listener.

Hence the temptation, when relating a dream, to point up, embellish, elaborate 'interestingly': adding to compensate for what, inevitably it seems, is lost in the telling. But in my dream, as soberly described above, the one and only intense emotion, the access of sick dread, short-lived yet piercing, is amply justified. It has its objective correlative: a planned and imminent suicide.

Given that feeling of fear and dread, no matter how fleeting, reason would suggest that the suicide, explicitly voluntary, should be abandoned. But then, as we have all seen, dreaming has its reasons that reason knows nothing of. There are things in dreams that the dreamer recognizes as unquestionable, irrevocable; there is no quarrelling with them. In the present case the assumption is that euthanasia has been legalized; and, like it or not, or having no feelings either way, there is, in the dreamer's mind, 'no going back'.

The disordered futon is noted in passing, and similarly the falling asleep hand in hand; the latter touch is represented as officially recommended, thus fending off any hint of what the literary critic might consider 'hideous sentimentality'.

The dash to the post office, through the dark night in the back of a darkened van, and the ignominious return – comical in retrospect – have been played down, if anything, in my account. These events too were undergone patiently, without surprise, consternation or resentment. To the best of my knowledge, only the figure of the 'manageress' has been tampered with: made a slightly larger, more intimidating presence than she actually was. Perhaps I have it in for her because she appeared to have it in for me? Or so I think – and think less certainly as the days go by and the dream settles and sets into its written record, as though it were no dream but a minor piece of recent history.

Schopenhauer has claimed that when in some ghastly dream, we reach the moment of maximum horror, it awakes us, thereby banishing all the monstrous shapes born of the night. The moment of plainest comedy or ludicrousness can have the same effect.

In a later dream my son-in-law, Toby Buchan, persuaded me to join him in a rugger match. I was aware that playing rugger in one's eighties was unusual, but I felt perfectly fit. The only difficulty was getting hold of suitable footwear. The weather was ideal, the game went well. The ball came into my hands, I pretended to punt it over the heads of advancing adversaries, then dashed forward, feinted again, making more progress, and passed the ball expertly to one of our side. Afterwards I tried to find out who had won. Otherwise accommodating as well as salubrious, the dream was disinclined to say. What mattered was the game, not who won, who lost.

'I am worn out with dreams': W. B. Yeats. A ridiculous idea! As for sex – you must be dreaming!

'It's only a game!' Of games and gamesters ... Musil's Ulrich, the brilliant so-called man without qualities, having been put in his place by hearing about 'geniuses of the football-field or the boxing ring' (1930), would have been rendered speechless by the news that a footballer had been offered a £2 million contract for his autobiography (the title already written: *My World*). Young Mr Beckham, reported as extremely excited by the project, says that much of the book will concern the World Cup of 2002 – a competition, as I remember, in which the England team performed abjectly: footballers with feet of clay. There needs no ghost-writer come from Grub Street to tell us this.

Incidentally, after England's goalless draw with Nigeria, a cheery BBC pundit assured us, in case we hadn't moved with the times: 'It's the scoreline that matters, not the game.' And no doubt it's the £2 million and the author's name that matter, not the book.

David Beckham is recorded as divulging apropos of his first son: 'I've a definite sense of spirituality. I want Brooklyn to be christened, but don't know into what religion yet.' Somehow spirituality has leaked out of the word 'christen'. It seems the ghost-writer will be kept busy earning his ghost-living. A 'Key to all Religions' would come in handy all round.

More and more I must sound like the old dodderer in Flaubert's *Dictionnaire des Idées Reçues*: 'Let me tell you, sir, that I knew tricycles when they had only three wheels.'

Sir Antony Jay puts a brave face on the lack of respect computers show for proper names, though he wonders what the postman will deduce from the monthly statement of the knight's joint account with his wife addressed to 'Sir Antony Jay and Lad'. Next he learns he is paying an annual subscription to an esoteric organization named Friends of the Ear.

Three sayings I can't chase out of my head, and cannot see why. '. . . like the man who preferred reading the dictionary to any work of fiction – not much story, but at least he could understand every word' (Paul Bennett, 1998); 'a radical theory I had always held but dared not openly formulate: that boredom in the arts can be, under the right circumstances, dull' (Gore Vidal, 1968); 'Are you in pain, dear mother?' asks Louisa, to which Mrs Gradgrind replies, 'I think there's a pain somewhere in the room, but I couldn't positively say that I have got it' (Dickens, 1854). Admittedly the last serves as a negative description of rheumatoid arthritis, where the pains move around unpredictably but the sufferer always knows exactly where they are at any given moment.

'I hope that you may be prepared to speak on the telephone soon to one of our current University students, and to use that opportunity to discuss with him or her the latest developments in the Faculty of English, including our plans for the new building.' This comes from a personal letter signed by Professor Dame Gillian Beer, King Edward VII Professor of English Literature at the University of

Cambridge. Fair enough. What I take amiss is the closing (and not too elegantly phrased) paragraph: 'As someone who has studied, and I hope enjoyed, English at Cambridge, your support of the Campaign is crucial in this final phase.' I was a student at Cambridge and writing for *Scrutiny* (remember it?) when the future Professor Dame sported rompers.

The current student, he or she, hasn't materialized as yet. Perhaps the word has got around at last that I'm a cantankerous old skinflint.

A reader of *The Times* confides that a children's charity has sent him a single chopstick. He can't manage a pair of them, and wonders what he is meant to do with one. An answer comes nine days later from a Chinese gentleman living in Hong Kong: the Chinese are served with single chopsticks whenever they eat crab, using the chopstick to push out the meat in the claws and the legs. Somewhere there must lurk a charitable thought, or a childish one.

Whether in acknowledgement or as inducement I cannot recall, but one charity sent me a sheet of address stickers. Undeniably useful, though a pity the name was rendered as E. N. Right. Have accumulated quite a stock of aliases: of less avail to me nowadays than even a widowed chopstick.

When we were living in Alexandria in the late 1940s we had an arrangement with a young beggar-girl strategically stationed in the vicinity of our flat. For a regular and modest donation, she chased away any other beggar who accidentally intruded on her territory, uttering savage cries. Apart from the latter – 'Those who beg in silence starve in silence', cited in Kipling's *Kim*, is said to be a native proverb – her behaviour was impeccable.

Quite the opposite of what happens here and now. Give to one of our highly organized charities and you are a marked man, you will find scores of others snapping at your heels, you are a certified soft touch.

As your afflictions mount up, some of them decidedly weird – is there no end to them? Well, yes, there is – don't lose heart. Think of those who are worse off. If that doesn't work, contemplate the American basketball star: 'I've never had major knee surgery on any other part of my body.'

In *The Devil's Dictionary* Ambrose Bierce observes that 'die' is the singular of 'dice', and that we so rarely hear the word is due to the prohibitive proverb, 'Never say die.'

A reader of *The Times*, describing himself as being of a generation for whom grass was for cutting, coke was kept in the coal-shed, and a gay person was the life and soul of the party, tells how relieved he was to find in a certificate of insurance issued by Lloyds TSB that some things hadn't changed. Under the heading 'Words with special meanings' came the gloss: 'Death means loss of life.'

That this was indeed a special meaning was confirmed by other readers, one of whom had bought an insecticide which she supposed would lead to the death of fleas, only to learn that one application would kill 'all adult fleas for up to three months', while another mentioned a can of fly-killer bearing the notice that it had not been tested on animals ('No wonder it did not work'). A third, in possession of a can of fly-spray that 'kills bugs dead', was left wondering what other state could possibly result.

Later we hear of a tin of paté offering the advice: 'Best pressed on bottom' (some variety of Gentlemen's Relish, perhaps?). And – a sign no doubt of our compensation culture – a sewing kit bearing the warning: 'Please be careful. This kit contains a small component with a sharp point (needle).'

Have passed the festive season, from Christmas Eve through to New

Year reading and reviewing a heavy-hearted study of suicide. Quite invigorating. Enhanced by a bottle of light tongue-tingling Clairette de Die (pronounced 'Dee', please note).

In a lecture of 1864 Ruskin expressed the hope of seeing before long libraries stocked with 'chosen books, the best in every kind, . . . broad of margin, and divided into pleasant volumes, light in the hand, beautiful, and strong.' This fine sentiment is quoted in Tim Hilton's *John Ruskin: The Later Years*, a book I persuaded Southfields Public Library to acquire, pleasant and beautiful and strong, of 680 pages, which I can only with pain support in both twisted arthritic hands.

The Broadcasting Standards Commission has ruled that it was (and is) not offensive to call the Queen a 'bitch' provided the epithet comes from a black man – since 'bitch' is acceptable street slang referring to a woman, and HM is a woman. The BBC confirms that the black comedian in question 'was using the term as it is used in rap music to mean "woman", and not as a term of abuse'. Some black community leaders are surprised to learn that rap is empowered to transform the long-established meanings of words, while the comedian himself, insufficiently appreciative of the intricacies of political correctness (and perhaps of the pre-eminence of his human rights), now states that he 'made an error'. How daring, how heartening, if the illustrious bodies mentioned above could also have second thoughts. But they can hardly be said to have had first thoughts.

In a different context – *Times* journalists being clever about social class, a supposedly dead horse that runs and runs without a touch of the whip – the Queen is described as 'a German who likes small dogs'. Given that we aren't all mad keen on the Germans, and some of us incline to treat small dogs with nervous derision, the expression might seem likely to cause offence. But no, it simply constitutes a non-judgemental class indicator acceptably articulated by a quality journalist in a quality broadsheet. (Off with his head!)

'Crumbly' and 'wrinkly' aren't very pleasing – compliments to the mother who countered by referring to her children as 'pimplies' – but preferable to the euphemistic 'experientially enhanced'. (As the man said, let's have some new clichés.)

'Words ending in –ess should be used with caution,' *Chambers Twenty-First Century Dictionary* tells us. ('Spineless' for instance?) Also 'Avoid using *man*'. That's something of a handicap, isn't it? But 'Avoid the term *handicap*'. Or just avoid this dictionary.

In 1926 H. W. Fowler objected to the use of 'their' in lieu of the logical 'his' or 'her'. The issue remains unresolved, says Burchfield in the *New Fowler* of 1996, but 'their' now passes unnoticed except by those trained in traditional grammar, 'and is being left unaltered by copy editors'.

'Inaccuracies can be subsumed as an inevitable part of postmodern uncertainty, or play, one or the other or both,' asserts the narrator of A. S. Byatt's *The Biographer's Tale* (2000). In the same novel: 'I told her quite truthfully that I was helping someone with their research.' The someone is another woman. 'How useful the increasing acceptability of the slightly incorrect use of the plural possessive.'

The Penguin *Literary Guide to London* informs us, of Frognal Gardens, Hampstead, that 'Labour politician Hugh Gaitskell (whose wife ran off with Ian Fleming), lived in No. 18'. In fact it was Gaitskell who had an affair with Ann Fleming. No sweat – libelling the dead doesn't count as libel.

In *The Times* of 23 September 2000 a picture of a skimpily clad, pouting young woman is captioned 'Sir George Young, who resigned from the Shadow Cabinet, at home in Wiltshire.' Sir

George didn't resign because of . . .; he resigned in order to stand for the post of Speaker in the Commons – as reported on the facing page, which carried a picture of him, looking just like himself, at home in Wiltshire.

There was a time when people working in the world of print sought to get things right, factually, semantically, grammatically. No one remarked on this, it was taken for granted, it didn't enhance the sales of books or the reputation of newspapers. The logical conclusion, I imagine, was that getting things wrong wouldn't have any effect either: no one remarked on it, it was taken for granted.

'Die Leidenschaft bringt Leiden,' Goethe noted: passion brings suffering. Psychologists in the United States have discovered (how?) that passages such as 'he undressed her slowly . . . then took her gently over the crest' greatly reduce a woman's will to practise safe sex. (Not, as you might have thought, to practise sex.) Now, it appears, publishers of romantic fiction are facing calls to print health warnings on book covers. By leaving out details such as the rustle of a condom packet, writers of romantic fiction, it is claimed, 'create negative attitudes towards the use of contraception and perpetuate the myth of being "swept away" by romantic love': thus the *Independent on Sunday*, 22 October 2000.

Mills & Boon hasten to plead that their books are 'more about romance rather than sex' (the passage quoted above makes one think of water-skiing in the nude), and that 'being too explicit is not something we encourage' (the rustling of condom packets is all too explicit). Joseph Brodsky has commented that 'Schmaltz is flesh of the flesh – a kid brother indeed – of *Schmerz*.'

It is rather saddening to learn that being swept away is a myth, but good that details are given their due weight, and even better to hear that what we read affects what we do, or do not do.

In an essay, 'That our desire is increased by difficulty', Montaigne reflects on the enjoyable and arousing verbal games that spring from the decent, even bashful language we use when speaking of amorous matters. In Proust, Swann's 'do a cattleya' is an example. Even the jaded roué, says Proust's narrator, finds a fresh pleasure if the woman in the case is – or is thought to be – 'difficult', and one has to initiate proceedings by rearranging the orchids pinned to her bodice. Something Edenic there, the very first love-making, in a prospect of flowers.

'Bashful': Montaigne's word is 'vergogneuse', which survives in modern French only in the substantive 'vergogne', generally preceded by 'sans'. In English, 'shame' – that discomfiting word – exists chiefly in such phrases as 'no sense of shame' and 'what a shame!', and in the adjectives 'shameless' and 'shameful'. Perhaps a trace of a lost meaning, an almost lost virtue, lingers on in 'shamefaced', originally 'shamefast'.

Finding his young son in the hayloft with the milkmaid, the farmer berated him: 'Next you'll be smoking!' An old joke which the Zeitgeist has rendered unfunny and even unintelligible. The point is neatly confirmed by Simon Leys in *The Angel and the Octopus* (1999) where he cites an English magazine as reporting that in a crowded railway compartment, 'a couple who had been engaged in passionate kissing for some time eventually came to perform full sexual intercourse under the impassive eyes of the other passengers'. It was only when the satiated couple pulled out their cigarettes that their hitherto silent co-travellers reminded them firmly that it was most improper to light up in a non-smoking compartment.

'I was the palace whore': *Times* headline, 9 September 2002. In the *Observer* Parisoula Lampson describes her life in one of Saddam Hussein's palaces, 'where she was lavished with jewels, cars and clothes'. And to hell with grammar.

*

It must be a dream, a bad dream. 'A masterpiece ... it has wit, erudition, golden dialogue' (*Observer*); 'Beautifully written ... there is not a single ugly or dead sentence here' (*Sunday Times*); 'A great popular novel and a plausible candidate for the Pulitzer Prize' (*Guardian*); 'The work of a real writer, following his own path, despite the pressures of fame. He's not doing it for money' (*Evening Standard*); 'Sentence for sentence there is nobody to match him ... an incredible achievement' (*Mirror*); 'If there's a better book this year, with truth, fantasy and a touch of erudition combined in prose which really does leap off the page, I'll eat my hat' (*Express*); 'A fine novel, deep and intriguing, worthy of its bald, bold language and biblical allusion ... a literary evocation of the diabolical to compare with Goethe and Gogol' (*Times*).

Page after page of panegyric, all to do with a novel rhymingly entitled *Hannibal*, by Thomas Harris. I must be dreaming, it can't be real, can it? Then, 'The most significant sequel since *Paradise Regained*' (*Independent*) – that clinches it, it has to be a blackly comic dream.

Stand up anyone who hasn't written a book about Sylvia Plath and Ted Hughes ... You, go to the bottom of the class!

'A survey reveals that nose-picking, burping and passing wind in public are now commonplace.' Another small belated consequence of the death of God. Once there was only one real, big celebrity; now we have thousands of tiny ones. The same is true of role models, or 'icons'.

Happy those early days, when ... when oral sex meant a messy, foreign, slightly absurd, teeth-clashing version of kissing. Or at worst talking dirty.

A Frenchman is brought in to rescue the Millennium Dome

(impossible task for any mere human), an American to resuscitate the London Underground, a Swedish coach to revive English football. What do we offer in return? An eight-year-old girl comes from the Ivory Coast in hopes of a better life in this country, and is tortured to death.

'Difficilis, querulus, laudator temporis acti . . .' It is amply attested to that old people are convinced things are getting worse all the time. On top of this predisposition, it is perfectly possible that some things are getting worse all the time. For one thing, there are more things all the time, or more things are brought to our tremulous attention.

In times past (which one certainly wouldn't want to praise unduly), things went unspoken, were left unsaid, there weren't so many words around. (There was no incessantly chattering television, among other things.) 'Having words' meant that the grown-ups were fighting – something kids used to dread. And no doubt still do, although quite a few of them have only one parent.

To be not without honour in one's home town! Some while ago a kindly resident of Leamington Spa sent me a cutting from the local freesheet, *The Observer*, hoping it would amuse me: 'As you see, we have not forgotten you, but we haven't quite remembered you either.' The cutting concerned the building which once housed my old school and is now being sold off. 'Famous past pupils,' the item read, 'include inventor of the jet engine Sir Frank Whittle and poet B. J. Enfield.'

Amusing? I am no longer sure. The May 2002 issue of *The Oldie* prints a letter from a Canadian reader laying into the magazine's columnist, Enfield Snr (father of Harry Enfield, a television comedian). Halfway through the diatribe, 'Enfield' mutates abruptly: 'Enright comes across as a very unpleasant man indeed, and I think he should take his gutter journalism elsewhere.' The letter writer must have been blinded by rage. (Or could he

conceivably have been out to kill two birds with one stone?)
Someone at *The Oldie* was thoughtful enough to insert '[*sic*]' after
'Enright', but not everybody understands what *sic* in square brackets
betokens.

My horoscope, given to benign protectiveness against a hostile
world, has gone over the top. 'The reason you can't do certain
things is because those things are of no importance.' Can they all be
of no importance, those many things, steadily increasing in number,
I can't do? All I need to do, it emerges, is be true to my 'essential
nature'. Which is to be unable to do certain things, like dress myself
without help.

Somebody loves me, though. British Telecommunications is
offering to convert my existing phone line into two high-speed
digital lines. Just the thing if 'you want to access the Internet and use
the fax or make phone calls at the same time'. Forget that fifteen
minutes of fame – here's a whole lifetime of *importance*. Moreover,
American Express remind me that they have written to me in the
past, inviting me to become a Cardmember. 'Usually I wouldn't
follow up such an invitation in this way,' the Director of
Membership declares, 'but I feel that you may be an exception. You
see, we'd like you to apply for Cardmembership.' So much so that
they have prepared a short application form which requires little
more than my signature. 'If you are too busy or occupied to
complete lengthy forms, you are precisely the sort of person for
whom the American Express Card was designed.' It is also designed
for 'those at a stage in their life when they expect efficiency, respect
and a willingness to please'. How enormously gratifying!

Should the application form fall into the hands of someone not
named thereon, obviously it is not valid. Such persons should call
Customer Services for an application of their own. This takes some
of the gilt off the gingerbread. As does a little lapse in efficiency:

'Staement queries will be answered immediatly, no matter what time of day or night.' A couple of *sics* in square brackets called for.

Matthew Arnold spoke of those 'who have laboured to divest knowledge of all that was harsh, uncouth, difficult, abstract, professional, exclusive; to humanize it, to make it efficient outside the clique of the cultivated and learned, yet still remaining the best knowledge and thought of the time, and a true source, therefore, of sweetness and light'. An excellent definition of humanist criticism, one might say: in some respects, to some extent, describing the intentions of book reviewers in the media and of others down to – or up to – the composers of jacket blurbs (unprincipled as these individuals often are, in a good sense as well as a bad). Also, negatively, an account of what goes on in some university departments of English, among the cliques of the harsh and abstract, the professionally cultivated and exclusive.

One may suspect a persistent – if attemptedly hidden – discomfort: among academics more than a few would prefer in their heart of hearts (can't come much closer to humanism than that) to be humanistic, if claim is to be laid to some sort of faith, by choice a vague or mild-mannered one, calling for no more approval or disapproval than they and their acquaintances for the larger part entertain without thinking. For instance, when they sit down with a book in the evenings, maybe a book they are reviewing for the relatively popular press, for that real though elusive figure, the common or general reader.

Of course sweetness and light will have to go – or at least scurry into the background – for there is a limit to one's daring. Bitter and dark are our watchwords, not without reason. Humanism must accommodate a deal of inhumanity. Hence one of the charms of literary theory, which far more smoothly averts its gaze from discreditable practices. In fact the question doesn't arise: for all the tough talk, 'theory' is another Phantom Aesthetic State.

*

But this is best left to those who know – and know all the better because they have a life elsewhere: above all, academics who teach 'theory' or at least make knowledgeable and qualified obeisance to it, and also happen to be successful satirical novelists. And foremost among these gifted persons is (as I write, alas, was) Malcolm Bradbury. 'Double agents' we might call them, or if this sounds inaptly sensational, they might be seen as having their cake and eating it, an achievement that demands an outstanding degree of smartness. Sir Malcolm, be it noted, founded a celebrated creative writing department in the University of East Anglia, thus promoting the birth of numerous authors rather than plotting the Death of the Author.

I begin to grow confused already, so allow me to quote the fictional young hero of Bradbury's egregiously artful and crafty novel, *Doctor Criminale*, as he muses on his undergraduate years at, so it happens, the non-fictional University of Sussex. 'It was the Age of Deconstruction, and how, there on the green Sussex chalk downs, we deconstructed. Junior interrogators, literary commissars, we deconstructed everything: author, text, reader, language, discourse, life itself. No task was too small, no piece of writing below suspicion. We demythologized, we demystified. We dehegemonized, we decanonized. We dephallicized, we depatriarchalized; we decoded, we de-canted, we defamed, we de-manned.' The upshot was that he no longer liked writers or their work. His education 'had proved to me conclusively that all literature had been written by the wrong people, of the wrong class, race and gender, for entirely the wrong reasons'. All this de-molition in three short years of de-learning.

To which I would append the more sombre and weightier words of Elaine Showalter (*London Review of Books*, 1 November 2001), to the effect that the habit of expressing ideas in a highly conventional idiom – or jargon – rules out the ability to write with clarity and force, and even to hold opinions at all. 'Graduate students are trained to write the received English of the academy and learn to suppress whatever flair, individuality and humour they had when they arrived.'

Postmodern: the very description of nullity, of the indisputably indescribable. All it suggests, if that isn't putting it too strongly, is that something comes after something else – as indeed most things do. And, as if expressly so designed, the clean contrary of Arnold's programme.

On a more mundane level: 'What everyone has in them, these days,' Martin Amis writes in *Experience* (2000), 'is not a novel but a memoir.' And 'The present phase of Western literature is inescapably one of "higher autobiography", intensely self-inspecting . . . No more stories: the author is increasingly committed to the private being.' The way things are going – *higher* autobiography? – before long every author will bear the pen-name Will Self.

We tend to believe what we read – despite proud protestations to the contrary – at any rate when the subject is one we know little or nothing about. Odd, that when the subject happens to be something we do know about, we often come on quite amazing inaccuracies.

On the front page of the *Daily Telegraph* Arts and Books section, Paul McCartney, interviewed by Roger McGough about his book of poems, says that his English teacher at A-level, 'a lovely man', 'had studied under F. R. Leavis at Oxford'. That's funny. I studied under Leavis, at Cambridge.

The story in Francis King's autobiography of how I smashed down a door in some foreigners' club in Tokyo and was consequently kicked out of Japan (such a pity!) after only a year there. Now this story, a total fabrication, has resurfaced in an important-sounding compilation entitled *Japan Experiences: Fifty Years, One Hundred Views*, published by the Japan Society. This is a subject I know – or would know – something about, and it never happened. I didn't smash any door, nor would the university I taught at worry much if I had; I completed my three-year contract in reasonably good shape, and was invited to renew it.

No one will believe King's story, says the editor of *Japan Experiences* breezily, a former British ambassador to the country, when I remonstrate. A truly diplomatic response; but Borges was nearer the mark in claiming there is no one who is not credulous outside his own area of knowledge.

Dreamt a truly happy dream: the Inland Revenue had sent me a repayment order for £110. The pleasure this gave went on and on in the dream. When I checked the following morning I found that the actual sum, received three weeks earlier, was £111.98. Pretty close.

In age there is more rejoicing over a refund of £110 or so from the Inland Revenue than over a publisher's advance of £250,000 or more. Well, more chance of rejoicing.

'The conquest was a technical conquest,' said the critic Herbert Howarth of Eliot's poetry back in 1965. 'But one result of technical conquests is likely to be that the technician inculcates his views with his craft.' 'Female smells in shuttered rooms': one of the poetic 'Observations', this may have affected the beguiled youthful reader as fresh and indefinably stirring, but later came to indicate something rancid in writer and reader. (A contrast with the sparkling lines nearby about the roses having 'the look of flowers that are looked at'.) More distasteful, more often quoted (does it make us feel special?) is the arrant generalization, 'Human kind cannot bear very much reality.' True, reality has murdered so many of them. More humane, kinder to humanity, is Milosz's drawing back in a late poem: 'Yet like others I repeat the socially acceptable words,/ for I do not feel authorized/ to reveal a truth too cruel for the human heart.'

But then, 'If Eliot wished to live quietly, succeeding in avoiding notice, living and partly living, without making his life a continual allegory, then he had a right to. There was pain, there was dignity, finally there was happiness. Let it go at that.' There is no decently dismissing this delicate summing-up, by Philip Larkin in a review of Peter Ackroyd's life of Eliot. There are realities humankind shouldn't be expected to bear, whether for the greater refinement of the soul or the production of great poetry.

In spite of some widely reported instances to the contrary, and thin, embarrassed and petulant sounds from one corner of the Zeitgeist, it is probable that the vast and unreported majority of mothers do care for their offspring, and care passionately. What prompted this risky speculation (who am I to talk, etc.?) was reading about a kind of antelope, *Antilocapra*, whose preternatural shyness and swiftness of flight testify to a time when predators were exceptionally menacing. As also does the dams' habit of eating the faeces of their young and drinking their urine, so as not to leave any betraying smells behind.

One may for some time have suspected that in the sphere of literature quality was a discredited concept. Now Professor Catherine Belsey of the University of Wales, Cardiff, has confirmed this in the plainest and most peremptory fashion. To the question *What is the future of English Studies? Does it have a future?*, she replies: 'I'm sure it has an enormous future, especially since the old canonized literary model has been diffused into a much wider study of cultural texts. Because we no longer ask, as our first question, how good a work is, but instead what it can tell us about the culture that produced it, we now have a great many new texts to read.'

That's to say, literature doesn't matter. The interview is printed in the Autumn 2001 issue of *Literature Matters*, the newsletter of the British Council's Literature Department, edited by Hilary Jenkins, the Council's Education Manager, who conducted the interview with Professor Belsey.

What does matter is our old friend 'theory'. *Do you think everyone has accepted the inevitability of theory now?* 'Certainly in this country the young feel that they need to draw on theory to read well. What we call theory is in the end an account of the relationship between human beings and language, and so between a reader and a text.' *Can you see what might come after theory?* 'In a way, if theory is about how we read, it's hard to imagine a world without it.' (Go on!)

Later in the interview Hilary Jenkins asks the Professor how she would describe the relationship between writers and critics. 'I think they might be well advised to pursue their own trajectories and ignore each other ... Book reviewing is the last resort of the value judgement. And too often the criteria of judgement seem to boil down to whether the book would be a good read on a train journey. Plot, character, suspense, structure, and whether its heart's in the right place: the values, in fact, of the nineteenth-century novel.' (Good heavens, we can't have that sort of thing going on!) Then a confusingly worded question, *Do you think writers confuse critics and academics?* 'I understand that confusion. We academics are too willing to get on the committees that award prizes. We should not be making judgements about contemporary writers ...'

Finally, *How do we raise the social profile of English Studies?* 'We need to get on TV. I've been unearthing feminine images of Hamlet in the nineteenth century. The material would make great television, but how do I start publicizing it? We need a committee, structures, strategies. Would this come within the remit of the British Council, I wonder?' (Suddenly the unworldly Professor needs a committee. As for the British Council, one wonders what does or rather what doesn't come within its remit.)

The back page of the periodical bears the usual health warning: 'The views expressed in articles are not necessarily those of the British Council', but was the British Council under any necessity to print this shameful, shameless, self-regarding tosh? (Not to mention dereliction of – absurd notion – duty.) In a halfway sane world vacancies would be arising in the staff of the University of Wales and the British Council. We must content ourselves with the thought that those whom a nerveless intelligentsia is disinclined to judge should be left to condemn themselves. Except that in this postmodern or whatever age there is no such culpable behaviour as self-condemnation.

In *Mind the Gaffe*, R. L. Trask's new guide to (or against) common errors in English, we are urged not to confuse the words 'principal' and 'principle'. Professor Trask tells us that he has just seen a document from the Committee of Vice-Chancellors and Principals in Britain 'in which the phrase "principle applicant" occurs more than forty times'. This, he concludes, 'is deeply embarrassing'. It certainly ought to be.

In the year 2000 the Department of Education destroyed 48,000 posters distributed nationwide to promote literacy classes, because of spelling mistakes, 'vocabluary' and 'though' (for 'through'). This was worse than embarrassing since the reprinted posters cost £7,000 of public money. The Department chiefs, too important to concern themselves with niceties, cast the blame on illiterate proofreaders.

Or their secretaries. In September 2001 a careers website reported that 110 customers seeking this employment contrived to misspell it in fifteen different ways, including 'securtery', 'sacratery' and 'secretie'.

The Do-Not Press describes one of its books as 'a dark *noir* mystery'. Foreign expressions confer a certain *cachet* or prestige, but should always be accompanied by a plain honest English equivalent. 'The problem with the French is that they don't have a word for entrepreneur': President Bush is supposed to have said this to Mr Blair regarding the decline of the French economy. (Are these Bushisms authentic or the work of hostile – or, come to that, friendly – spin-doctors?)

I have just heard tell of a bilingual wedding invitation, the English version ending with RSVP, the French with the words 'Réponse souhaitée'.

Some relief from one's petty anxieties (should one address her as Doctor or Mrs or Ms? How does one pronounce that Tamil name?) comes from hearing of the agonizing dilemmas faced by other people. A busy Welsh banker living in Amsterdam has acquired an English butler to look after his domestic affairs. Everyone in Amsterdam speaks English, and the banker, though he has learnt Dutch, never uses it. His butler doesn't speak Dutch at all well, and the banker is thinking of paying for him to have lessons in the language. Is this the correct thing to do?

The authority on social correctness retained by one of our leading broadsheets rules that it is not essential for the butler to learn Dutch since 'as purveyors of an impenetrable language, the Dutch have long mastered our tongue'. On the other hand, it would be 'an extremely effective social gesture', helping to integrate the butler into the life of the Netherlands ('Live?' proclaimed Prince Axel, literary creation of the penurious nineteenth-century French count, Villiers de l'Isle-Adam: 'The servants will do that for us'), and moreover he might on occasion need to deal with persons whose English is not of the usual high standard. There is no indication of the butler's views on the question. He knows his place, and it's not in the newspapers.

Oh no? A fortnight later the butler appears in the same column, explaining with admirable lucidity that his problem is different and more delicate. The people he concerns himself with are mostly accomplished speakers of English, but they have difficulty understanding him because of his Scouse accent. He is proud to be a Liverpudlian and wouldn't have dreamt of trying to 'talk proper' when working in Britain. However, he now thinks he should learn to speak English more clearly. At the same time, he is worried,

especially at his age, that if he changes the way he expresses himself
he may turn into a figure of fun.

The judicious mentor, no doubt happy to exercise his rare skills,
advises him to seek tuition that will render his speech 'less parochial'
and more readily intelligible to the Dutch. This would entail diluting
the Scouse flavouring without losing it altogether. A little easier, I
imagine, than attaining proficiency in Dutch. But what a treasure
this butler must be! (If he exists.)

Fears have been circumspectly voiced that the English are becoming
a mongrel race. Yes, a bit scruffy, snarling at passers-by, getting
kicked in the ribs. Still, better mongrel than pure-bred. But don't
count on such multicultural joys in store as bare-breasted clog-
dancers or the Kama Sutra arranged as pantomime. Religion is the
better – at least the bigger – part of some cultures, so watch out.
You may come to wish that multiculturalism resulted in nothing
worse than culturelessness.

Addressing themselves to my 'literary estate', Gale Research Inc.
thought me more dead than I was. In a communication dated 7
December 2001, Cornhill Direct thinks me more alive than I am.
'Dear Mr Enright, Why is this date important? 1st January 1941. It's
your birthday of course. So let me wish you Happy Birthday in
advance.'

There is, Cornhill Direct informs me, another reason why that
date is important. 'Based on your age of 60, a £14 monthly
premium gives you £2,189 of life cover.' In fact, I'm far too old to
avail myself of Cornhill's Senior Security Plan. Reports of my
(relative) youthfulness have been exaggerated.

The young man at Cornhill who takes my call shows no surprise.
Information on likely clients, he says, is supplied by an independent
market research outfit. Nor does he show any remorse, though he
expresses temperate regret that I am excluded from the Senior

Security Plan and the 'welcome gift' that goes with it. He promises to remove me, the supposed me, from the Cornhill computer.

A picture in the *Times Literary Supplement* is captioned 'A Ukrainian woman catches pigeons for her Christmas dinner in Kiev's central square.' A Ukrainian subscriber writes that Ukrainians do not eat pigeon, and the caption ought to read 'A Ukrainian woman feeding pigeons in a Kiev street.' Let's hope a British ambassador assured Ukrainians and pigeons that no one would believe the printed story.

In 1936 a German scholar pointed to Heine's shallow knowledge of the German language and the disfiguring effect of residual Yiddish. For example, the opening line of 'Die Loreley': 'Ich weiss nicht, was soll es bedeuten' – a true German would have written 'Ich weiss nicht, was es bedeuten soll'. The scholar omitted to mention that even then Heine still went astray, deluding himself that 'bedeuten' rhymed with 'Zeiten'.

A little later, the poem – so popular, so German, that it couldn't possibly be ignored, or written by a Jew – was represented as a folksong. Far from defective grammar and false rhymes betraying its infelicitous provenance, these were evidence of authentic folksiness. Heine must have written better than he knew: he invented an instant tradition.

Where did that endearing television comedy, *The Last of the Summer Wine,* find its name? Someone, it now emerged, was claiming that the phrase, in French of course, occurred somewhere in Proust's extensive oeuvre. Some ten years before, when my wife and I were revising the translation of *À la recherche du temps perdu* in accordance with the second Pléiade edition of the text (1987–9), we liaised with Rowena Skelton-Wallace at Chatto and Windus, an intelligent and helpful young woman. It was she who rang to tell me of this development and invite me to call in at her office. There she showed me a large, roughly shaped cylinder of rock on which, she said, every word ever written by Proust was inscribed, somewhat in the manner of a compact disk. Would I like to take it home and study it? As Proust's long-time English publisher, Chatto would be tickled to know where and in what connection the phrase came, if indeed the claim was true. A fascinating little job, I thought, searching for the words 'le dernier vin de l'été' or whatever. I tipped the heavy rock into a rucksack, slung the latter over my shoulder, and set off for home.

There the dream ended. A happy dream, invoking happier days, linking the apparently artless and lowbrow with the ostensibly rarefied and highbrow.

'T. S. Eliot was gay – official': on front cover of *The Oldie*, January 2002. 'How gay was Hitler?': on front cover of the *Times Literary Supplement*, 11 January 2002. That ought to put paid to this sad perversion of a once cheerful little adjective.

At a time when dysphemisms have put euphemisms to flight, and a spade is called the gravedigger's accomplice, it is rather nice to catch a glimpse – just a brief glimpse, you understand, one does not hold with ivory towers – of the parallel universe of Billy Collins, the American poet, in which a history teacher is solicitous to protect his pupils' innocence. The Ice Age, he tells them, was really just the Chilly Age when everyone had to wear sweaters, the Stone Age turned into the Gravel Age, named after the long driveways common at the time, the Spanish Inquisition was simply an outbreak of questions such as 'How far is it from here to Madrid?' and 'What do you call the matador's hat?', and 'The War of the Roses took place in a garden,/ and the Enola Gay dropped one tiny atom/ on Japan'.

(And what is called a playground is a ground where children play innocent games. It is noted in passing – if not by the teacher himself

– that when the bell rings for playtime, the pupils soon divide into bullies and bullied, and the strong torment the weak. Parallels meet.)

Extract from Wandsworth Social Services, Occupational Therapy Assessment Report:

'CULTURAL CONSIDERATIONS (including Language): No cultural considerations mentioned during initial assessment.'

'COMMUNICATION: Mr Enright communicates his needs and wishes clearly in English. He wears reading glasses and is able to write with difficulty using a pen with a thick grip.'

'ACTIVITY: Mr Enright is able to independently transfer on/off his bed ... Mr Enright does not comply with Physiotherapist's recommendations to use a walking frame.'

'LEISURE Interests/Hobbies: Mr Enright writes books and visits the local library regularly. He watches television and enjoys reading.'

Therapy has developed its own dialect. Nouns officiate as verbs, transitive verbs as intransitive. 'He fatigues easily', 'mobilizes slowly', 'adapted cutlery to be provided, after trialing different types'. The Department is obliged to send the client a copy of the assessment. Seeing oneself as others see one – in this case a tall Valkyrie-like young woman, bossy but pleasant with it – gives the subject a weird sensation, as if a short sharp earthquake has jolted him out of his normal cubby-hole in the universe. Not necessarily a bad thing.

Slowly I am approaching the end of the final draft of this book. Bits of it, I think, are rather good; I say as much to a couple of old friends who drop in. That night I dream the book is finished, falling naturally into three parts. I pass it to an unidentified, distinguished-looking person, prominent in the literary world, so the dream lets me know, and influential among publishers. Having read it, he tells me with icy clarity: 'The first part is boring. The second part is rather more boring. The third is more boring still.' The words ring in my ears as I awake.

In *PN Review* 138 John Killick, once editor of a small press, quotes an aspiring genius who came his way: 'Here is Part One of My Diary; with all its imperfections I make the claim that it contains Great Poetry. I dare aver a memorable verse on each page. I am prepared to make cuts where necessary, and why I sent you so many pages is because I like the ninth verse on page 140. Page 170 is the climax of my poem, though I have much to say afterwards, and will continue to do so until one day I am too good not to be published.' Mr Killick remarks that in his experience letters of this sort are always written by men. Presumably women have been too oppressed in the past and are too mature in the present to permit themselves any such excesses of self-admiration and advertisement.

Years ago our daughter planted an apple pip in a pot and it grew into a sapling, too tall for her flat. It was transplanted to our garden, where it flourished, amazing everyone privileged to see it, and in the fullness of time bearing apples, more and more each year. My wife, a confirmed nature lover, doted on it, and it thrived on her ministrations. This year strong winds blew the tree over. When my wife tried to lift it up, it fell back on her, knocking her to the ground. 'Red in tooth and claw,' I said, as she washed off the blood. I said it to myself. (But for my wife, not a word of this journal would have been written. Literally – yes, a proper place for that weighty adverb – not a single word.)

Time, perhaps, to look again at Musil's warning that you cannot be angry with your own time without harming yourself (a warning Ulrich never allowed to interfere with his pleasures), and at Horace's complaint about complaining, on this occasion invoked by Matthew Bramble in *Humphry Clinker* (1771), and passed to me by Tobias

Smollett's biographer, Jeremy Lewis. Thus: 'There is another point, which I would much rather see determined; whether the world was always as contemptible, as it appears to me at present? – If the morals of mankind have not contracted an extraordinary degree of depravity, within these thirty years, then must I be infected with the common vice of old men, *difficilis, querulus, laudator temporis acti*; or, which is more probable, the impetuous pursuits and avocations of youth have formerly hindered me from observing those rotten parts of human nature, which now appear so offensively to my observation.'

As I copy this out, the BBC announces a new sitcom: 'Reassuringly offensive'.

It never rains but it pours . . . One of the truest of clichés, elaborated in the soldierly words of our national bard: 'When sorrows come, they come not single spies,/ But in battalions.' Our much loved cat, sick with liver cancer, had to be taken on 'that last fated hateful journey to the vet' (a line of Gavin Ewart's), and put to sleep (another cliché, and euphemism – thank God for them). A few days later I slipped on the recently polished kitchen floor: lift-off was smooth; landing ungainly, and so a broken rib. (What can't be cured must be endured – which is a relief.) Then my wife had to go for an endoscopy; she always accompanies me on these hospital trips, and the least I could do was accompany her. We turned up at St George's, she the frail invalid, me the macho bodyguard. We were there in the unit for several hours, the waiting-room was stuffy. My wife sailed through the endoscopy. I had a dizzy fit, and had to be pushed in a chair to the thronging entrance hall, where flowers could be bought and cabs ordered, my wife trotting manfully behind the porter. Roles reversed; the female of the species more lively than the male. In age and sickness pride is repeatedly injured, which must be hard on those not already used to it, whether in waking life or in dreams. Happily my *amour propre* was never a passionate love affair.

Then something happened that almost made it, some of it, worthwhile. The young black cabbie allocated to us was sweet-natured and kind-hearted, above and beyond the call of duty or of any conceivable tip. (He didn't want one.) Every cloud has a silver lining? But this was an avatar, as if some aspect of deity had chosen that moment and that place to descend among us.

And this would be a good note to end on. On the brink of sudden happy tears.

– Were it not that life, or whatever, goes on. Colonoscopies show that my wife has a suspect ('pre-malignant') polyp. (As I write, it remains on bail.) A biopsy reveals that chemotherapy has left me rather worse off, the trouble having spread to the prostate. St George's hands me over to a new hospital, the Royal Marsden in Chelsea, where I receive a new name, 'Enbright'. (Soon rectified.)

Apparently I'm not up to any taxing treatment (fine by me), so they'll give me a dose of radiotherapy once a week. Am quizzed on my first visit by two incredibly beautiful and bright young women doctors.

(Time to finish writing a book, eh? A freakish excuse for wanting to stay alive. Must be genuine. What's it called? That's a funny title. Poor you. Injuries done to other things too, like language? Oh.)

– By shrinking the tumours the treatment may procure extra time.

– The treatment is time-consuming and tiring.

– Swings and roundabouts. It's a bit of a toss-up, you see.

(God is his own interpreter, and he may not like the sound of the book.)

The dazzling doctors – they seem to have all the time in the world – lead me through a lengthy consent form, detailing possible side-effects. As an erotic experience, out of the ordinary: '. . . impotence' (remember how Sima Qian got to finish his book), '. . . loss of pubic hair' (no occasion for public mourning).

Never a dull moment, hardly ever.

'Dr X will see you now': a smiling nurse leads us to a shining room. 'Please wait here.' After weeks of preparation, scan after scan, I am about to meet the much talked-of team leader. And in bounces Dr X, a middle-aged woman, waving a clipboard and beaming broadly. 'Splendid!' she cries, 'We are so pleased with you! Your PSA is way down the scale, far lower than we could have hoped for.' (PSA, I later discovered, stands for Prostate Specific Antigen test; the lower the reading, the brighter the outlook.) Could this be me, a well man? 'It shows how marvellously well the treatment has worked.'

Reluctantly, I hold up my hand: 'I'm sorry but I haven't had any treatment yet.' She freezes for a moment, then stares at the clipboard. 'You're not Mr Payne?' 'Well, no,' I start, but she has fled. 'Come back, Doctor,' I call after her, and 'Yes, yes,' I hear fading in the distance.

But she never did come back. Never. Just my luck, to alienate the boss at first contact – merely by not being happy Mr Payne.

Used to read the newspaper . . . Used to read the headlines in the newspaper . . . Used to read the first two or three words of the headlines . . . Have given up reading.

Expelled from the relative luxury of the RMH, the home of Dr X, and back at St George's, in the oncological ward. An ebullient old codger in the next bed has lost a pound coin during the night. The following morning he nags on about the coin to all who come within range. Eventually a nurse seeks to cheer him up: his wife will give him another pound. 'Dare say she would,' he booms, 'but she's dead.'

'There was things which he stretched, but mainly he told the truth': Huckleberry Finn's opinion of Mr Mark Twain. For all the allure of unhappiness, and its marketability, there will still be chroniclers tempted to alleviate the truth in the name of hope, even to submit a happier ending.

'And therefore, Reader, I am myself the subject-matter of my book: it is not reasonable that you should employ your leisure on a topic so frivolous and so vain. Therefore, farewell.'

Montaigne – with the nonchalance of a born gentleman – placed his address 'To the Reader', his adieu, at the very forefront, the beginning of his book.

INDEX